CH

D0786493

COMICS CONFIDENTIAL

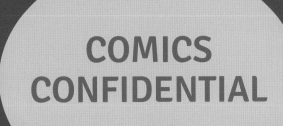

COMICS CONFIDENTIAL

THIRTEEN GRAPHIC NOVELISTS
TALK STORY, CRAFT, AND
LIFE OUTSIDE THE BOX

LEONARD S. MARCUS

CANDLEWICK PRESS

First edition 2016

Library of Congress Catalog Card Number pending
ISBN 978-0-7636-5938-7

16 17 18 19 20 21 APS 10 9 8 7 6 5 4 3 2 1

Printed in Humen, Dongguan, China

This book was typeset in ITC Stone Informal.

Candlewick Press
99 Dover Street
Somerville, Massachusetts 02144

visit us at www.candlewick.com

For George M. Nicholson—
agent, mentor, dancer, friend.
In memory.

CONTENTS

FOREWORD

Leonard Marcus's dizzying array of achievements as a writer and historian in the field of children's literature has made him a revered figure. The fact that he is also modest, discreet, low-key, and a nice guy in person adds to his being one of my heroes.

The thoughtfulness and appreciation that went into his latest collection of interviews, and his use of the phrase "Life Outside the Box" in his subtitle, inspire these thoughts from my own experience with the graphic novel as the author of *Stitches*.

I long had it in the back of my mind to write a memoir of my youth. For years I could only imagine this as an extended work of prose, which is to say that it was doomed never to become a book. Drawing, for me, is as natural as breathing, but prose, quite frankly, is hard. When I discovered the graphic novel form, it made my fingers itch to render my memoir in panels equating to frames in a movie. It gave me the opportunity to expand my visual storytelling from the necessarily tight strictures of the thirty-two-page picture book format in which I had long been working.

What, then, did I make? It's not a picture book, not a film, and I certainly wouldn't call it a comic. Rather, it shifts around among all these genres like a blob of mercury, and I felt that shifting motion while I worked. It was an exhilarating experience. I could not lay claim to having done anything truly new, but, to me, it felt fresh.

As Leonard recounts in his introduction, a war of words continues to rage over what this sort of book should be called and how it should be classified. I like to think of *Stitches* as "slow film," but that term certainly doesn't apply to every sequential visual narrative. Who knows what term will finally take hold? All I know is that it was thanks to this new form that my book was, at long last, born.

Deciding where to slot *Stitches* caused challenges (I once found it in the "Crafts" section of Barnes & Noble with the books on sewing.) and at least one major debate when it was nominated for a National Book Award in the young adult category. Some saw *Stitches* as written for adults, while others saw it as a perfect book for teens. It must have been difficult for my publisher, W. W. Norton, to know exactly where to place *Stitches,* and it became upsetting when self-appointed "authorities" online blasted it for having been first issued as an adult book, then repositioned in the young adult category to give it a better shot at an NBA. They thought this was covetous. It was! Everyone wants to win a National Book Award. But the dispute was not about the quality of my book; it was about pigeonholing.

We must not denigrate the taxonomists among us. (They are there to tell us which drawer to find our socks in. This is important.) Nor should we ignore the concerns of marketing departments. What we must never do is listen to these folks while we draw and write. Art-making at its best is a confrontation with the mysterious and the irrational. If we listen to the people concerned mainly with classification or marketing, we end up not making honest and true works of art, but only *product,* rubber-stamped and made to fit into a prefab box that might as well be a casket.

In so many of the interviews in *Comics Confidential,* the artists, when asked what they were like as children, tell us that they were nerds. That is code for those who are born to a life perpetually outside the box.

Those who grow up on the periphery of normality are like astronauts forever circling the earth in their own private capsules. It is a lonely life, but in fact, the view from up there is better, broader, and more all-encompassing than the average person's. When nerds come to accept and appreciate their condition, when they begin using their typewriters, computers, and art supplies to pass the time in their dark passage, and when, above all, they take advantage of the view, they rule.

I applaud Leonard Marcus and all of the sweet people (some of them my friends) whom he has chosen to honor by interviewing them for this book. It's like a homecoming for life-travelers who are forever in orbit, seeking new forms in which to express themselves.

David Small

INTRODUCTION

A funny thing happened to some of the millions of kids who grew up over the last few decades devouring comic books and the daily cartoon strips they read in their local newspapers. They became comics creators—artists and writers who, instead of outgrowing their childhood love for word balloons and spindly action drawings, chose instead to pour their hearts and souls into the genre. Making comics became their career. Even more than that, it became their life's work. While some realized their dream by taking jobs at big commercial publishers like DC and Marvel, others pursued a less clear-cut path. They simply sat down and started to write and draw, often in the beginning just for the entertainment of their friends. Before long these independent, or "indie," comics creators began to meet one another at comics shops and conventions, at book fairs, and via the Internet. They inspired, challenged, and fed off one another. To their amazement, they discovered that artists and writers like themselves—and fans too—were all around the world. In time book publishers noticed what they were up to as well. Without quite realizing it, these indie artists and writers had invented a new art form—a new kind of book for which people at first did not have a name. By the early 2000s, the books were everywhere.

Because the new books (unlike traditional comics) were often a hundred or more pages long and because they generally told a story, some people began calling them "graphic novels." The label worked well enough—except for the fact that many of the books were not fiction but memoirs, histories, and other kinds of *nonfiction*. Even so, the name "graphic novel" had a solid, impressive ring that helped persuade the doubters—of which there were a great many at first—to give the quirky, at times wholly uncategorizable creations a chance.

In the United States, comic books had always had their critics as well as their fans. No sooner had the first ten-cent action-adventure comics appeared on newsstands during the 1930s than librarians and teachers raised the alarm. These well-intentioned naysayers feared that two-fisted tales about superheroes like Superman and Green Lantern might "overexcite" young readers. They considered comics a waste of the time that could be better spent on Caldecott and Newbery Medal winners. Children by the millions loved the comics anyway—and often read them in secret under the covers at night, when their parents thought they were asleep.

Opposition peaked in the 1950s when an American psychiatrist named Fredric Wertham published a best-selling critique in which he argued that action and horror comics encouraged young people to turn to a life of crime. The U.S. Senate held hearings to determine if this was true. Out of fear for what might result from the investigation, the publishers of comic books established the Comics Code, a self-censoring scheme that set strict guidelines for acceptable story content—and put a damper on comics creativity for years to come. Against the backdrop of this history of fearsome opposition, the new graphic novelists had their work cut out for them to win an audience—and respect—for their indie enterprise.

The turning point came with the publication of Art Spiegelman's *Maus: A Survivor's Tale: My Father Bleeds History* (1986) and *Maus II: A Survivor's Tale: And Here My Troubles Began* (1991), a harrowing comics-formatted saga about the artist's father's Holocaust experience. In 1992

Spiegelman received a Pulitzer Prize for his monumental work—unprecedented recognition that prompted many to rethink the old truism that nothing that looked even remotely like a comic book could possibly be a real work of art.

After Spiegelman's triumph, things began to change. Readers became increasingly aware of the graphic novel's long, many-stranded history. It was a history, they learned, which—in addition to *Superman, Batman,* and the like—included nineteenth- and twentieth-century Chinese illustrated *manhua* and Japanese illustrated *manga* tales; the newspaper strips of nineteenth- and twentieth-century Europe and America; the experimental wordless novels of the Belgian artist Frans Masereel and the American Lynd Ward; and from the 1960s and 1970s, the edgy "underground comix" of Robert Crumb, Spiegelman, and others. As the new books won broader acceptance and were given a place on public library and bookstore shelves, more and more creators and fans came to refer to the books by the simpler, old-fashioned term "comics." As this change occurred, the genre itself was changing: while a great many of the first graphic novels had dealt with nightmarish and forbidden fantasies, disturbing personal histories, and other "dark" material, now lighter, more playful books entered the mix. Some artists and writers even began to make comics for beginning readers.

Why did all this happen? One reason has to do with our living in a time when written communication is more fast-paced and tightly packed than ever before, and when visual images play an ever-greater role in how information travels. The creators of comics are masters of both these contemporary shorthand languages. They are, in fact, as knowingly in sync with the way we codify and share our thoughts today as anyone alive.

Another explanation may come from quite a different source: the intensely personal, even intimate feel of comics as an art form. Although comics are often published today in glossy commercial editions, they still retain much of the idiosyncratic, homemade appeal they had when indie artists were first cobbling them together on the fly, one hand-drawn frame and hand-lettered speech balloon at a time. No wonder comics creators and fans continue to see themselves as members of a close-knit—albeit global—community.

The artists and writers we meet in these pages are among the most talented comics creators working today. While nearly all are themselves lifelong comics fans, they came to their work by way of a surprising variety of backgrounds, including biology, computer science, filmmaking, painting, and acting. Not surprisingly, the stories they have to tell take off in an abundance of equally unpredictable directions.

Accompanying each interview is a one- or two-page comic created especially for this book, and a sampling of preliminary sketches and/ or manuscript pages. Each of these comics was made in response to the same open-ended invitation to produce a story about "the city." Just what city it would be was for the artist to decide. A city of the past, present, or future? An imaginary city? All were fair game. Why cities? Great urban centers with their diverse populations and feverish concentrations of big dreams and new ideas have a fantastic dimension all their own. As such, cities have captivated comics masters from Winsor McCay (*Little Nemo*) and Hergé (*The Adventures of Tintin*) to Will Eisner (*The Spirit*) and Bob Kane and Bill Finger (*Batman*). I was curious to see what each of the thirteen gifted storytellers in this book would do with the challenge. You will want to take your own close look at their singular responses. The stories they tell here about themselves are equally surprising and inspiring. Theirs are true stories from the labyrinth of childhood, school, and growing up; real-life tales of high adventure on the page and screen.

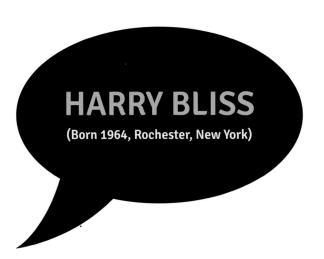

HARRY BLISS
(Born 1964, Rochester, New York)

Growing up, Harry Bliss saw artists everywhere he turned. Both his parents were artists. So were three uncles, four cousins, and a sister and brother. It was an uncommonly creative environment but also an emotionally lopsided one, with the usual hugs and kisses often in short supply when those around him got caught up in doing their own artistic thing. Another young person might have turned his back on the free-form artist's life and opted for a more predictable one as, say, a lawyer or dentist. For Bliss, however, the question was never *whether* to be an artist, but what kind.

In art school he studied the work of the illustrators he had loved as a child, starting with Richard Scarry. He sent fan letters to his artist heroes and when possible made pilgrimages to meet them. His sweetest triumph came when a letter to William Steig blossomed into a friendship that led, in turn, to his illustrating *Which Would You Rather Be?,* a picture book written by the creator of *Doctor De Soto* and *Sylvester and the Magic Pebble.*

Like Steig, Bliss became a *New Yorker* illustrator. Drawing for that sophisticated magazine gave him the chance to produce darkly humorous gags about childhood, family life, politics, and the people he observed all around him. The *New Yorker's* art director, Françoise Mouly, shared his passion for comics, and when she launched a company to publish comics-style children's books, she asked Bliss to create books for her list. He took the invitation as a chance to return to one of his first loves as a comics-crazed boy back in upstate New York, when, as he later recalled, "*Nancy* and *Blondie* spoke to me. I'd fall asleep with a paperback edition of *Pogo* open on my chest. I still have my plastic Snoopy doll. He sits on my flat files and watches me procrastinate."

I spoke with Bliss by phone from his home in Vermont on December 2, 2013.

. . . .

Leonard S. Marcus: What kind of child were you?

Harry Bliss: I was a child of extremes: very introverted but also really extroverted when I was trying to get the laughs. I loved making people laugh. That seemed really important to me.

People didn't show their feelings in our family. No one said "I love you" or even "How do you feel?" So my defense mechanisms got to be very strong. I don't think this was just true of our family, either. It was true of the neighborhood! It may have had something to do with the water. But my parents were very supportive of my interest in art.

Q: You grew up in a family of artists. What was that like?

A: Making art was something we all had in common. Art was the one thing we could all talk calmly about, without getting too overworked! My father painted for many years and was a graphic designer. In the sixties he did a cover for *TV Guide*. My brother, Charlie; my sister, Rachel; my uncle Harry; and my cousins are all artists. My mother, who is a master gardener now, painted watercolors when I was growing up. In our house we never thought about money, and no one ever told me to be a doctor or a lawyer. My parents were fine with me becoming an artist too, if that was what felt right. As a teenager, I spent hours in the evening sketching my parents as they watched *The Rockford Files* on TV. As the youngest, you become the observer.

Q: What kind of student were you?

A: In grade school I got a certain amount of recognition for my talent, and that meant a lot to me. Up until that point, school had seemed pretty dismal. We were living in Henrietta, New York, a lower-middle-class suburb of Rochester, and the public schools there were terrible. I spent hours in the public library and would take home armloads of art books and picture books. That went on right through high school.

Apart from that, I was a very rebellious teenager. I was the class clown and kept getting kicked out of class for disruptive behavior. My friends and I drank and smoked our share of the wacky weed! We laughed a lot. I didn't go to graduation, and I crashed the prom. I would do anything for a laugh.

Q: Did you read comics?

A: Absolutely. Our family collected comics and had tons of them lying around at home. I read lots of obscure things. For instance, I read *Creepy* and *Eerie* magazines. Or, rather, I looked at them, from panel to panel. As a young kid, I was not a big fan of the written word! I veered away from comics that required a lot of reading, like *X-Men*. On the other hand, an artist I couldn't get enough of was Bernie Wrightson, the illustrator of *Swamp Thing*! It was the same for Carl Barks's *Donald Duck.* At the same time, I was also reading books of Renaissance drawings. We didn't distinguish between "high" and "low" art in our house. It all excited us.

When I was thirteen or fourteen, I had a particularly interesting evening when my dad took us to the Rochester Memorial Art Gallery to see a show of original comic book art. There were drawings by Burne Hogarth, who drew the *Tarzan* newspaper comic strip, Charles Schulz, Frank Frazetta, Walt Kelly, and many others. My dad taught us how hard it was to do the kind of drawing that Walt Kelly was known for, which required such great hand control.

Q: Did you think about becoming a comic book artist yourself?

A: For sure. When I was ten or eleven, I would copy Mort Walker's comic strips *Hi and Lois* and *Beetle Bailey.* I don't know why I gravitated toward those strips. I do know that as I sat there with my little sketch pad and brush and ink, I wanted to get the same line quality as his in my drawings. A couple of years later, I did a sort of pornographic comic book for a friend of mine who lived up the street. It was full of busty women like the ones in *Conan the Barbarian.* I would drop each new issue off in my friend's mailbox. Around the third issue, his mom busted me. She said with a sneer, "I *saw* your comic, Harry." It was really embarrassing! I wish I had them now.

Q: What about a little later, when you went off to the Philadelphia College of Art? What were you thinking of doing?

A: By then I had discarded comics, not because I thought they were lowbrow but because I had become more interested in the great seventies illustrators, like Bernie Fuchs, and had decided I wanted to be a magazine illustrator like them. My first-year roommates included a guy from England and one from Vietnam, and a rich kid from Philadelphia who was a Deadhead. I was exposed to so much by them. It was a year of inspiration. We drew and worked and worked and smoked a lot of pot. After a while, though, I realized that the illustration department wasn't challenging me. I already knew a lot of what

Up, Up, and Away

by Harry Bliss

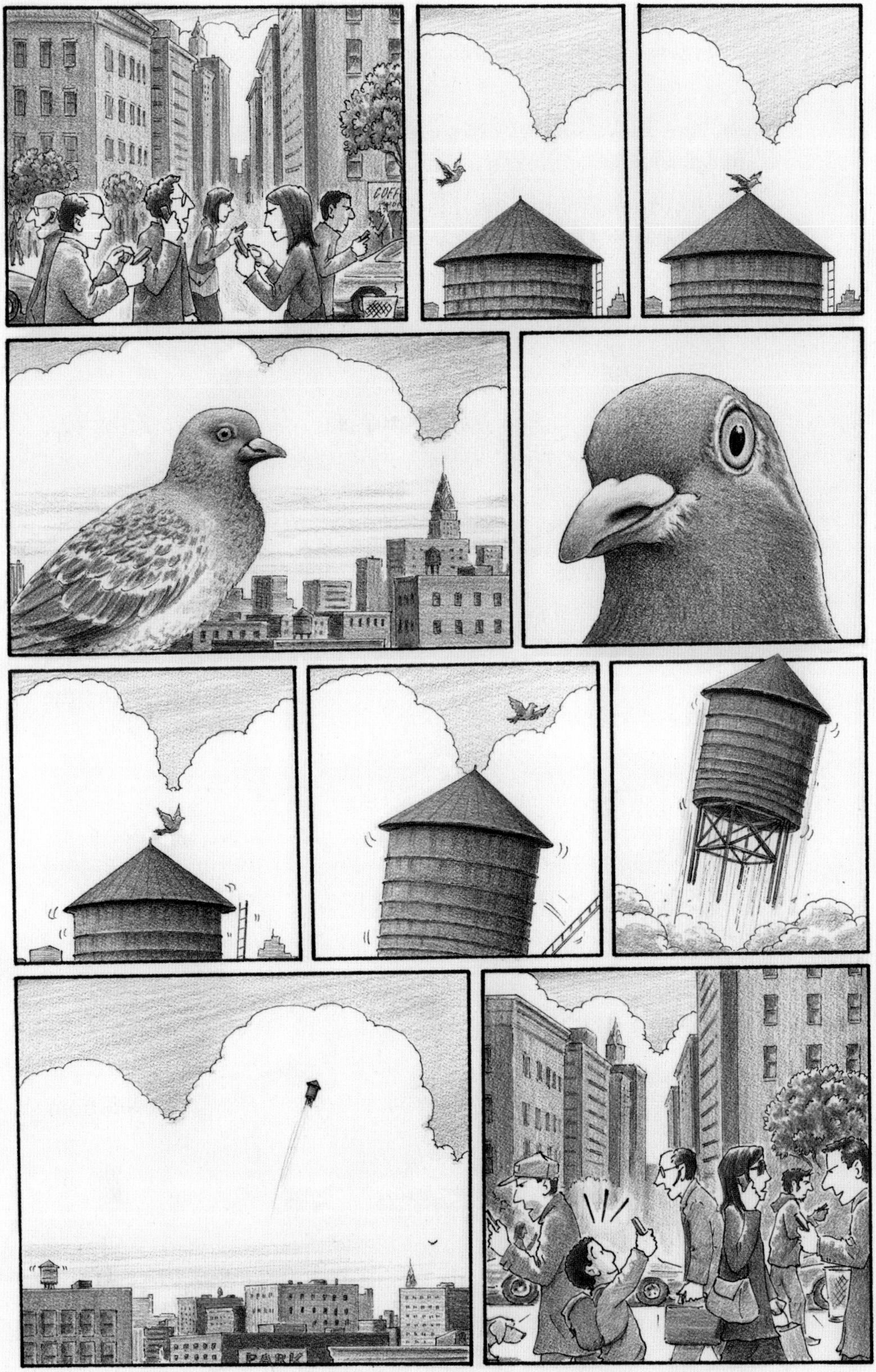
PARK

they were trying to teach me. So I left and went to the Pennsylvania Academy of the Fine Arts. The painting instructors there all had a studio at the school, so I could visit them after class if I wanted. That was a great experience too. But then I discovered girls and dropped off the planet for a while, left school, and became a father. About four years later, I got serious again and finished my studies.

Q: How did you become a *New Yorker* illustrator?

A: We had always had copies of the *New Yorker* at home, and I had always liked the cartoons and the covers. One of my favorite *New Yorker* artists was Charles Addams, who was so funny and dark and drew so well. A few years after completing my studies, I came across a book of Addams's cartoons, and I felt so inspired by them that I went home and made up eight or ten sample cartoons of my own and sent them to the magazine. This was in 1997. I received a note back inviting me to try some cover sketches. Not long after that, I had my first *New Yorker* cover published.

Q: How did you get started as a children's book illustrator?

A: I had written a fan letter to William Steig, and we began corresponding back and forth. This was not long after I had started drawing for the *New Yorker,* where he had been working forever. He put me in touch with his agent, and after a while I was doing my first picture book.

Q: You've said that William Steig is one of your heroes. What was it like to meet him?

A: I met Bill late in his life. He was terrific, still very curious at ninety-three. The first time we met, he asked lots of questions, wanting to know all about my family, where we lived—things like that. We had lunch at his apartment in a room decorated with remarkable hooked rugs he had made, beautifully designed with stunning colors.

Bill helped me rediscover the beauty of the unknown as it relates to drawing. He showed me how to let go of my insecurities and simply find joy in watching the ink hit the paper. I had become conservative about drawing, and it wasn't allowing me to reach the level of sincerity I wanted to achieve. Bill's late drawings were all about letting go and seeing what might happen. Where will this ink take me? What's next? I learned from him that drawing is all about growth and exploration.

Q: How is creating a comic different from making a picture book?

A: There's a lot more work in comics. It's a much slower process. I think of the panels as visual words. Each panel needs to be read, and as the artist you have to pay close attention to even the smallest detail in every panel so that the reader will too. There's an iconic comics visual language that I find really interesting and love to use. If a character is very nervous, I will throw in some "sweat lines." I like to use "walk marks" to indicate motion. Speech balloons make the characters' spoken words more immediate for the reader, more like action.

Q: There is something so obvious, or maybe guileless is a better word, about all those devices. Does that have something to do with why they are so much fun?

A: It's the fun of doing everything in an exaggerated, over-the-top way.

Q: What was it like doing *Luke on the Loose*?

A: It was a fantastic experience. The art director at the *New Yorker,* Françoise Mouly, is also the publisher of TOON Books, and she asked me to do a book for TOON. My son liked to chase pigeons, and it seemed to me that that was pretty much a universal thing. So I came up with the story, and with Françoise's help, I put the plan for the book together in just three days. That was the first time I told a complete story in comics form.

Françoise's husband, Art Spiegelman, also helped. He talked with me about what happens in a comic between the pictures: the parts of the story that you don't actually see and how they relate to the parts that you do see.

Q: How did you come up with your character Luke?

A: Originally, he was inspired by my son. But I wanted the boy in my story to be an African-American kid. I thought, "I'm sick of doing white kids!" I did a bunch of character studies for Luke before I felt I had him just right.

Q: What makes the comics format a good one for beginning readers?

A: I know that when I was growing up, I was intimidated by books that had nothing but blocks of words on a page. It was overwhelming to me, and I found the relief I needed in comics. Comics can be stepping-stone books for kids like the one I was.

Q: What inspired the comic you created for this book?

A: I've always been fascinated by city rooftops. I'm not sure why. Perhaps it's all the film noir movies I watched as a child. Water towers silhouetted against the cityscape are particularly interesting. Their antiquated forms are like rickety rockets about to take off. New Yorkers tend to look down at their devices these days and miss so much that is going on up overhead. For me, the city is best represented in what's above. Many of my *New Yorker* covers depict this point of view.

This early set of drawings, depicting a water tower that suddenly lifts off like a rocket, already has a pretty sly story to tell. But the comic gained in dimension when Harry Bliss added an assortment of human bystanders to the mix.

Q: What are you working on now?

A: I'm working on a graphic novel based on the true story of a young graffiti artist in New York City. He was sixteen years old back in the 1970s when he got caught spray painting inside Yankee Stadium. Instead of having him arrested, the owner of the team decided to make him a batboy. All these years later, he still works for the Yankees organization. It's a really interesting story.

For me, the most difficult part of the project has been figuring out how to break down the text: deciding which parts go in a narrative box, which lines of dialogue go with each panel, and so on. It's all very tricky and can take months. Then I'll have to decide on the drawing style, how realistic or loose the drawings should be. Then I will need to do lots of research on the Bronx in the 1970s—what the cars and hairstyles looked like, all sorts of things like that.

Q: Do you have a work routine?

A: Most days I get up and go to my studio. Typically I'm there from eight a.m. to six at night. Monday is "cartoon day" when I'll do a bunch of drawings to submit to the *New Yorker* in time for the magazine's weekly deadline. Wednesday through Saturday, I work on kids' books. I may take a day off but not very many.

In the past year or so I've become attached to a couple of pens I've discovered. One is a Montblanc Meisterstück and the other is one I picked up at an outdoor flea market in Moscow, a vintage pen I've yet to identify. I write and draw every day with these pens in moleskin journals: cartoon ideas, figures, notes, stories—journal entries and such. These pens and the way the paper responds to them is pure joy for me. I don't use the pens for my cartoons or any other work, just for the journals, but I'm sure I'll make the leap one of these days.

I've become very picky about papers, inks, pens. I simply won't draw if my supplies don't respond. Humidity in the air is very frustrating. I need very dry air in my studio for the graphic and ink to "take." It's all very intimate and personal . . . or maybe I'm just a control freak!

Q: Is there anything that you cannot draw?

A: Horses maybe. But I can pretty much draw anything from memory. In the comic I did for this book, "Up, Up, and Away," I looked at some reference photos of water towers, but I just made up the cityscape. One of the best pieces of advice I ever got from another artist was "Just draw." Don't get too caught up in technique. I found that suggestion very freeing.

Q: What do you like most about making comics?

A: As a comics artist, you are creating a whole new world. You open it up as you go, and in a way it opens you up. It's a very liberating feeling. I feel so fortunate to be able to do all the kinds of work that I do. I don't take any of it for granted.

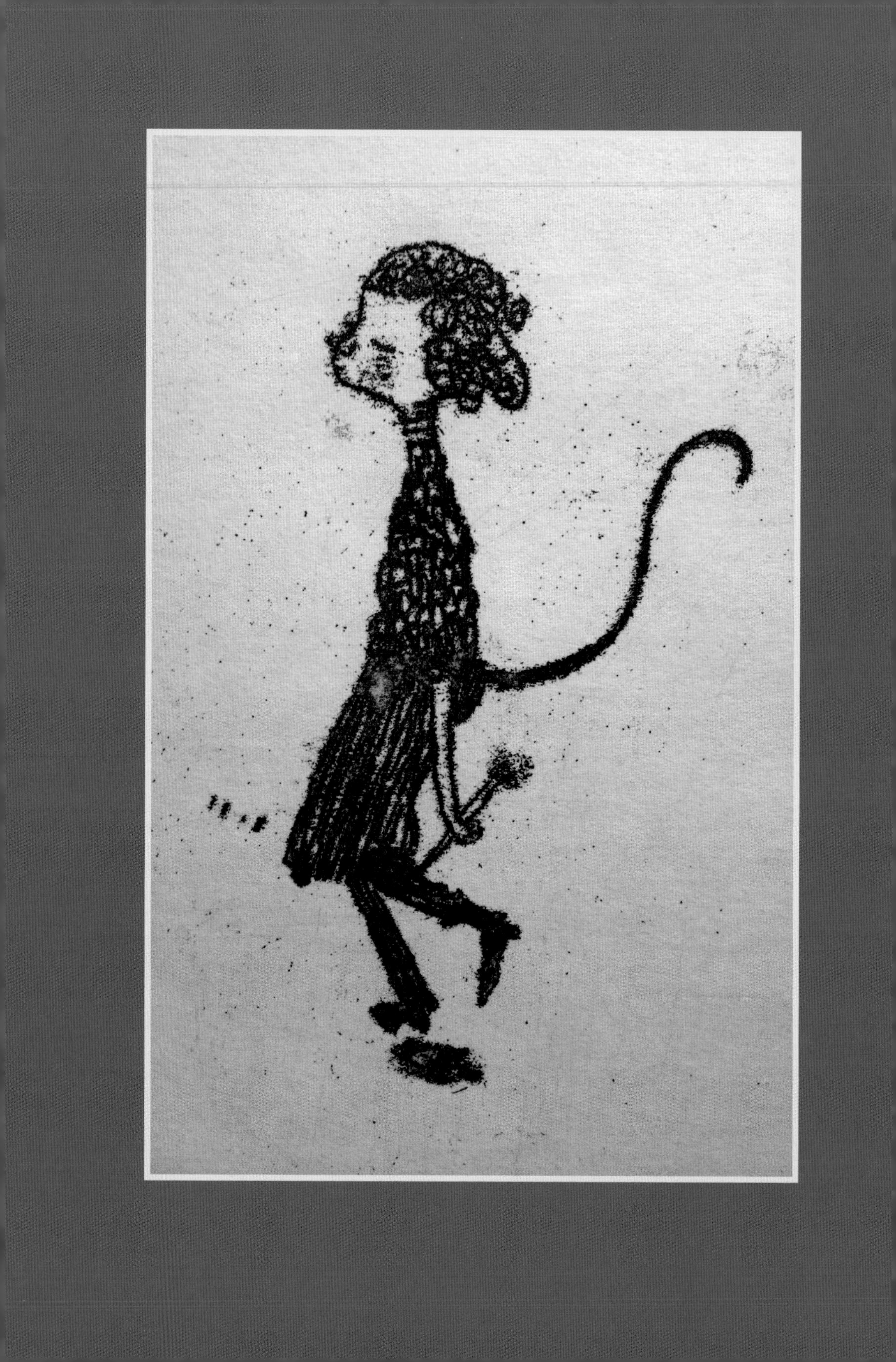

CÁTIA CHIEN
(Born 1978, São Paulo, Brazil)

Cátia Chien was born in São Paulo, Brazil, where her Taiwanese family owned a business, and moved to the United States as a high school student. Insects were—and remain—a particular passion of hers, and in the conversation that follows, Chien explains how a deep childhood curiosity about bugs eventually led her, by a path that at first surprised even her, to the work she does now as an artist. Insects, of course, inhabit a kind of miniature universe in our midst that can be thought to resemble an alternate world like the ones about which comics artists and writers have sometimes spun out fantastic tales. In somewhat the same spirit, Chien's artwork—her gallery paintings as well as her illustrations for picture books and graphic novels—take the viewer to a place that looks to be both familiar and strange. Her characters' adventures could be set in our world as seen from an unexpected angle or through some sort of special distorting lens; then again, they could be a dream.

Becoming a comics artist was not the original idea Chien had in mind for her art career. She saw herself as primarily a gallery and concept artist for animated films. But while she continues to paint and work on film projects (as well as picture books), she perhaps feels most at home in the highly collaborative comics community that gave Chien her first chance to publish her work. We spoke in the studio she shares in Brooklyn on January 13, 2014.

● ●

Leonard S. Marcus: What were you like as a child?

Cátia Chien: I was a daydreaming tomboy with perpetually skinned knees from falling off my bicycle! I spent a lot of time outdoors studying insects and exploring pockets of green in a city sprawling with high-rises. I was born and raised in a big city: São Paulo, Brazil. I didn't have a private backyard, but I lived in a condominium of eleven apartment houses with a park in the middle. There were these stocky short palm trees that housed swarms of the deadliest-looking caterpillars, all fuzzy black with red dots. All you had to do was shake a tree, and bugs would come tumbling down!

I grew up reading a lot of comics. The most popular comic book writer/illustrator in Brazil at the time was Maurício de Sousa. He was a big influence on me growing up. I liked his comics because they were fables about kids just being kids. My favorite of his comic book characters is a toothy tomboy named Mônica, who carries her blue stuffed rabbit by the ears wherever she goes. Her crew of friends range from a girl who can eat a whole watermelon in one bite to a boy named Cascão who doesn't take baths. I could relate to being a tomboy and playing with kids who were unique and different. Today I still feel the same love for slice-of-life stories like the ones told by Maurício de Sousa. That is the kind of story I go back to as a reader and that I want to tell as a writer/illustrator.

Q: Were you a good student?

A: Yes, I was nerdy: picture frizzy hair, glasses, a lab coat!

Q: Did you like to draw?

A: Not especially, but I got involved in doing crafts with my dad after school. He would make these gorgeous intricate paper-cut paintings, and I drew with him from time to time. But I was mainly into science. I thought I would grow up to be a biologist or an anthropologist. But after two years in college at the University of California, Santa Barbara, I changed my mind and left because I realized that I really wanted to go to art school.

It happened in a strange way. I had taken a college course in entomology—you see, I have always loved bugs!—and the teacher had us find an insect, study it under a microscope, and then paint it. I found a perfect specimen of a dead yellow jacket in a piece of rotten log. My final painting for this class was as big as one of the walls in my living room! I stayed up all hours of the night to finish painting a space cadet riding on the back of a yellow jacket. I found that I loved painting. This experience made me want to keep painting—and to become an artist. I dropped out of UC Santa Barbara, researched art schools, put together a portfolio, and after much nail biting and many sleepless nights got accepted to Art Center College of Design, in Pasadena, California.

Q: What was Art Center like?

A: It was rigorous, with so much work to do each day. A lot of us were pulling all-nighters to finish projects. It was hard, but it cultivated a level of professionalism and a strong work ethic that has helped me continue to do good work in my art life post-school. I made close art friends who, to this day, still inspire me to push my craft further. And it was there that I found my voice as a narrative artist. The teachers I gravitated toward were interested in visual storytelling and in comics, and they helped me to see that my paintings were like snapshots from a bigger story. Gradually, I realized that the art I most wanted to do was right for not only film but also comics.

Q: You completed your studies at Art Center in 2004. What did you think you might do after graduation?

A: Wheels were already set in motion to publish a book. Right before I graduated, Kazu Kibuishi and I set some time aside to put together a comic book anthology. Kazu is an amazing storyteller and artist. You definitely want him on your side if you want to do anything. He is one of the most hardworking artists I know! We first met when I was in high school, and when I got into Art Center, I introduced him to my art friends there. During my last year, we started thinking that with so many amazing artists around, why wait for someone to notice our work? Why not find a way to publish a book ourselves? We weren't thinking in terms of making money. We just wanted to have people see what we could do. So I invited my art friends Chris Appelhans, Khang Le, Jacob Magraw, and others. We gave ourselves deadlines and page limits and got to work. We called the anthology *Flight,* and by the time I graduated, it was done and ready to be shown. We got a table at the Alternative Press Expo—or APE—and that is how we found a publisher for *Flight,* which Kazu thought of as the first book in a series, the way manga are done in Japan. I created a story for the next volume of *Flight* as well. At about that time, I began to read more and more graphic novels— books by Art Spiegelman, Craig Thompson, Marjane Satrapi, Shaun Tan, and others. I also branched off into illustrating picture books full-time.

Q: How did that come about?

A: It was by chance that Kate O'Sullivan, a wonderful editor at Houghton Mifflin, saw my website and contacted me out of the blue. She had a story for me to illustrate. I took the project, and it became my first picture book, *The Sea Serpent and Me,* written by Dashka Slater.

Q: Were you doing web comics too?

A: No, I couldn't keep up. It seemed to me that people who did web comics were very prolific and very quick. They might do a new comic every day, which is extremely intimidating to me. I work much more slowly.

Q: How do you do your art?

A: It depends on what medium I am using, but to get ideas, I will typically start at the library collecting pictures for inspiration, which I then put together into a "mood board." Then I start doodling watercolor drawings on a piece of paper, just random shapes. As I continue sketching, I gradually find the shapes of my characters. To create the world in which they live, I use the same process, the only difference being that for backgrounds I typically like to sketch using graphite powder. These go from sketchy, blurry charcoal/graphite shapes to something more refined.

Q: Do you have a work routine?

A: Since I started working in a shared studio space here in Brooklyn, I have kept pretty regular hours. Normally I get up at eight a.m. and head to the studio after I get a cup of tea. It takes me about forty minutes by subway to get there. So depending on my workload, I'm

WATER

BY
Cátia
Chien

FROM
A POEM
BY
MICHAEL
BELCHER

ONCE

I MET

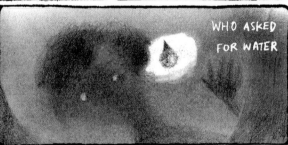

A TREE SPIRIT

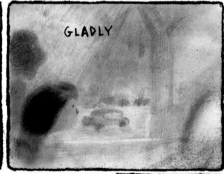

WHO ASKED
FOR WATER

I

GLADLY

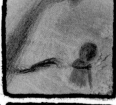

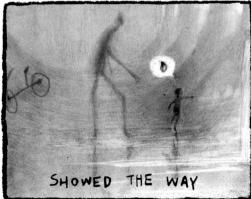

SHOWED THE WAY

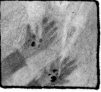

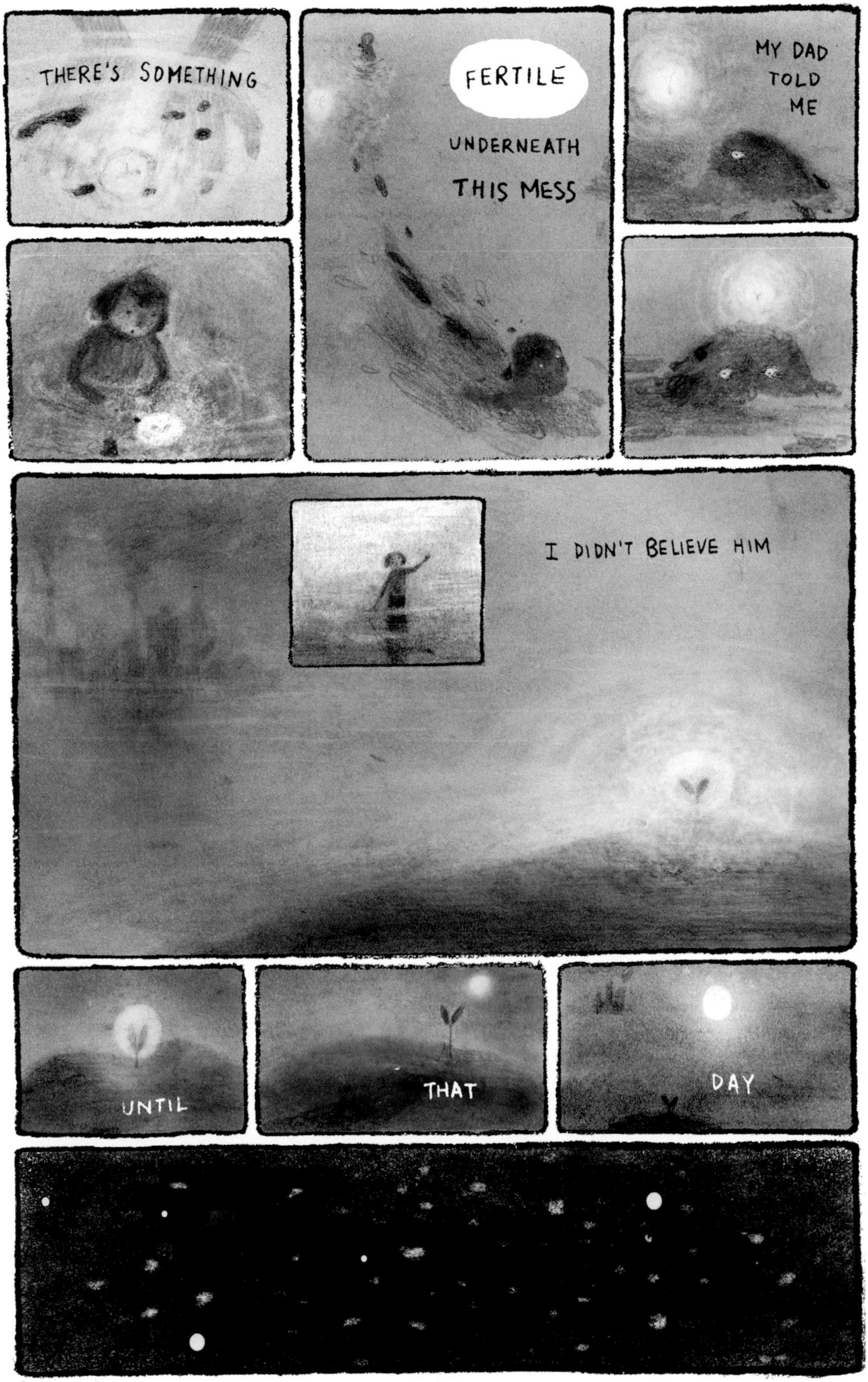
THERE'S SOMETHING
FERTILE
UNDERNEATH
THIS MESS
MY DAD TOLD ME
I DIDN'T BELIEVE HIM
UNTIL
THAT
DAY

normally a ten-a.m.-to-seven-p.m. person at the art studio most weekdays.

Q: Are there some things you cannot draw?

A: Oooooh, so many things! For instance, I can't draw hands or feet. My friends make fun of me because my characters end up having double-jointed wrists and claw fingers. Oh, and I can't draw a really good horse—they end up looking like pudgy oversize dogs, but I keep trying!

Q: Do you think your interest in bugs has influenced your art?

A: Now that you mention it, I guess some of my characters are insect-like. Some of them are small, buggy-eyed, and have very skinny legs and rounded bodies. Also, insects are misunderstood, and I imagine that more than a few of my characters feel a bit misunderstood in their world.

Q: Do you identify with them in that way?

A: Certainly moving to the U.S. and not being able to speak English at first, I dealt with stereotyping and feeling a sense of not having a voice, of being invisible. I think the same is true for so many insects who are misunderstood, so, yeah, I do identify with them in that way. Spiders, for example, can be seen as pests, and it's easy to see why that can be the case. They can be scary and intimidating-looking. But come to find out the orb weaver spider, for example, is crucial to gardens and is a docile creature that would be highly unlikely to bite. Still, I will get notes from editors who are afraid of upsetting parents, telling me not to draw a little child standing so close to a spider, even if the spider is meant to be an orb weaver. It's unfortunate that misconceptions are perpetuated in this way.

Cátia Chien draws in a wispy, kinetic, soft-focus line that instantly whisks viewers into a mysterious realm of shadows, dreams, and spirits.

Q: Your comic for this book, "Water," was inspired by a poem by Michael Belcher. What drew you to that poem and the story it tells?

A: The story is about the tension between nature and city, which I find fascinating. I love to look at abandoned city spaces that nature has reclaimed. In "Water," I wanted to show that nature—as personified by a mysterious tree spirit who meets a city dweller—will always take root, wherever and whenever the conditions are right. It is a hopeful story about second chances.

Q: What do you like best about making comics?

A: I love so many things about making comics! There is so much to consider: for instance, how a reader's viewpoint emotions are affected by where a character is placed within an image. Then there are the colors, the placement of the speech balloons, and the choice of type. You are always guiding the reader's eye by your choices. And then there's the fact that even though these are still images, there's a clear sense of the passage of time. I think that's magical! It's such a rich world of possibilities.

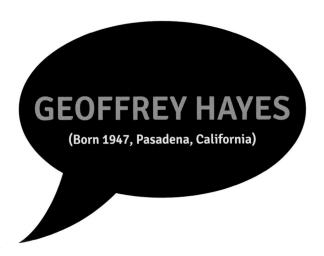

GEOFFREY HAYES

(Born 1947, Pasadena, California)

A rt and storytelling have always been central in Geoffrey Hayes's
life. As a grade-schooler and later as a teen, he and his younger
brother, Rory, loved many of the same toys, books, movies, and comics.
Together they formed a two-boy fantasy factory, filling their free time
at home with projects that included picture stories, puppet shows, post-
ers, and plays. When they were not collaborating, they took turns being
each other's number-one fan.

The restless Hayes family called San Francisco home, but never
remained at any one address for very long. They changed neighbor-
hoods with such dizzying regularity that the brothers found it impossible
to make friends. This brought the two of them even closer together. So
did the onset of puberty, which Hayes recalls as an earthshaking and
intensely creative time: Banding together, the brothers "fortif[ied]" their
"inner world," inventing distinct personalities for each of the stuffed
animal toys they had first played with a few years earlier, developing
the toys into a cast of characters for the stories and plays they wrote
as a team. "We [weren't] the first siblings to share an imaginary universe," Hayes observes, although at the time everything they made and

did together felt uniquely their own. "Our world," he says, felt "private and sacred." It was all good training for the brothers, who both went on to have notable art careers, although Rory's was cut short by lifelong emotional difficulties that eventually spiraled out of control and ended in a drug overdose.

Hayes's illustrated stories about wee, wide-eyed furry creatures are often described—and have sometimes been dismissed—as "cute." Hayes has a thoughtful response to this suggestion: "I still believe," he says, that "we can never have too much sweetness in the world, and am pleased to contribute what I can." The books, he notes, are not *only* cute. The drawings are as much about *drawing*—the challenge of seeing how much action and feeling can be packed into a few spare lines and daubs of color—as they are about toy bears and mice. Ultimately, readers care about Hayes's characters not because they are adorable but because they are small, doughty adventurers making their way in a big and scary world. In future books, Hayes suspects, he may take a different direction. "I'm finding increased inspiration in bucking trends and pushing the envelope. I feel I've done more than my share of 'nice.'"

Hayes had just moved to North Carolina from his longtime home in New York City when we spoke by telephone on November 4, 2013.

● ●

Leonard S. Marcus: Did you enjoy growing up in San Francisco?

Geoffrey Hayes: As a kid in the 1950s, San Francisco was a great place to be. The downtown seemed exciting. The liquor stores sold comic books! That is where my brother, Rory, who was just eighteen months younger than me, and I bought most of our comics.

Q: Did you have favorites?

A: I liked funny animal comics like *Donald Duck, Mighty Mouse,* and *Felix the Cat* and funny stories about kids like *Little Lulu* and *Sugar* *and Spike.* Rory and I weren't big on superheroes such as Superman and Hawkman, although we read them, too, just because we liked comics so much. We especially liked anything that was a little odd or off-kilter. If one of the Disney artists drew Donald Duck with an exaggeratedly big round head, we noticed and liked it.

Q: Did you talk about comics with your school friends too?

A: No, this was all between my brother and me. My brother and I drew for each other. We drew before we could write. We did two wordless books together when we were very young. One was about a devil who came out of the sewers through a manhole to terrorize people. That's all I remember about that one! The second book was about a character called Little Miss Lady who was constantly being chased by someone or falling off a cliff. Later we did stories for each other. We had a teddy bear who became our main character. He is the early incarnation of Patrick and was even named Patrick after our own Patrick Henry School. As kids you don't go too far afield! But we made an entire universe populated with stuffed animals.

Q: How about your parents? How did they feel about comics?

A: They felt that as long as we were reading, comics were fine. They were more concerned that we not see certain movies, like *Psycho.* Of course, we went and saw it anyway! Both my parents were amateur artists, and while neither of them encouraged us to become professional artists, they didn't discourage us either. They supported whatever we wanted to do.

As a matter of fact, when I was very young, I thought I wanted to be an actor. Then at about age twelve everything changed, and I realized that comics were my first love. Something about the format fascinated me. I've always loved sequential storytelling. A comic is almost like a movie, and as the artist you are the actor *and* the director *and* the designer. You get to create an entire universe all by yourself.

Q: Were you the class artist?

A: I was hardly a child prodigy, but, yes, the other kids were aware of my talent. I just loved to draw, and as I kept drawing, I got better over time.

Q: You said once that a flashlight was your favorite childhood toy.

A: It was one of them. Rory and I had a big flashlight with different colored filters. It was all very theatrical. We'd project images on the wall and create haunted houses in a room using the flashlight for special effects. We got a lot of mileage out of that flashlight.

Q: Did you and your brother remain close?

A: We did. As Rory got older, I was in New York and he was in California, so we didn't speak as much. Unfortunately, he got into drugs at that time in his life, and he finally OD'd when he was in his early thirties. By then he had become well known in the underground comix movement. His stuff was very dark—so dark that it even surprised me. But Rory was not a particularly dark person to be around, though he was certainly a troubled person. He was one of those kids who came into life with the short end of the stick. He was very emotional, and he had to wear glasses from the time he was a toddler because one of his eyes was crossed, which is very difficult for a young kid. He had a lot of strikes against him. The darkness in his comics was a creative way for him to release his demons, to get out the anger that he felt.

Q: After art school, you worked for a time in an architect's office. What did you do there?

A: I had studied mechanical drawing in school and was a good drafts-man. Among other things, I drew floor plans. The precision that goes into that kind of drawing has always fascinated me.

Q: The spreads in your books are so beautifully structured. Is your skill at that somehow related to the kind of drawing you were doing in that office?

A: Oh, yes. My favorite part about doing the comics is creating the page layouts, planning the movement of the characters throughout the page, keeping everything clear and readable while also being as inventive as possible.

Q: Did you always want to make funny comics rather than, say, scary ones?

A: I've always considered myself a humor writer. Humor comes easily to me, and it's what interests me. By the time I was ready to start a career, Marvel superhero comics were very big, and the funny ani-mal comics I had grown up with were fading away. So I turned to making picture books and beginning readers, both genres in which it was all right to be funny. But I have always embraced my shadow side, too. During the same period I was formulating my first stories for children, I was swooning over Bernie Wrightson's horror comics and wishing I could draw well enough to emulate them.

Rory and I would love anything that was odd or quirky about a character. When we were young men and both living in New York, for instance, we would see street vendors selling these weird balloons with feet and a face. The character was called Swissy Mouse. We

MISTER BEAR MAKES HIS MOVE

by GEOFFREY HAYES

DARN CITY!

DARN CROWDS!

DARN NOISES!

IF ONLY I HAD A QUIET PLACE IN THE COUNTRY WHERE I COULD COOK AND PLANT A GARDEN!

OOOF!

S'CUSE ME!*

HEY! YOU AREN'T THE ONLY ONE ON THE STREET! JERK!

THAT DOES IT! I'M OUTTA HERE!

FAREWELL, BIG NOISY CITY! OFF TO RETIRE IN PARADISE!

*CITY SPEAK FOR "GET THE HELL OUT OF MY WAY!"

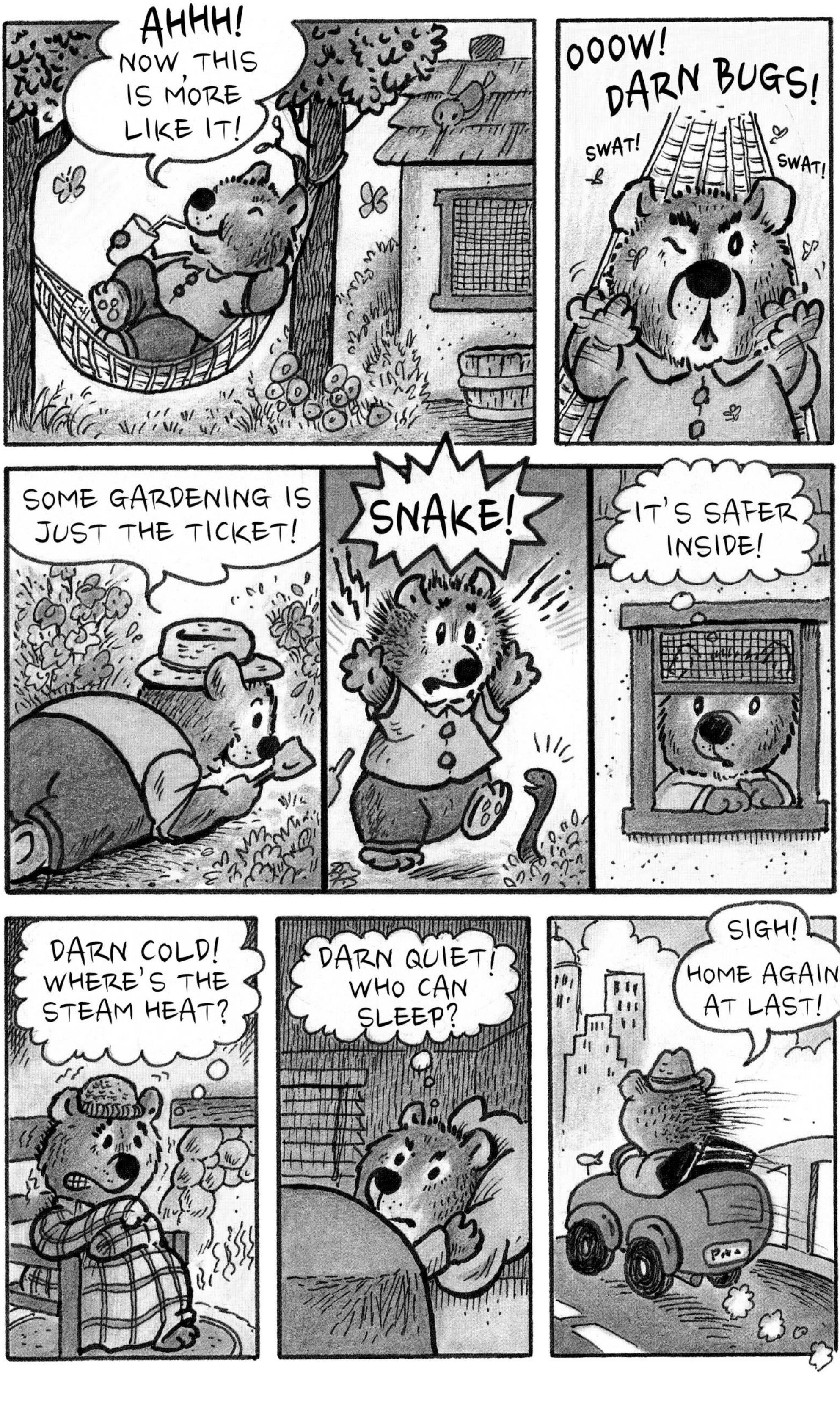
AHHH! NOW, THIS IS MORE LIKE IT!
OOOW! DARN BUGS!
SWAT!
SWAT!
SOME GARDENING IS JUST THE TICKET!
SNAKE!
IT'S SAFER INSIDE!
DARN COLD! WHERE'S THE STEAM HEAT?
DARN QUIET! WHO CAN SLEEP?
SIGH!
HOME AGAIN AT LAST!

would just stand there and watch the balloons bob up and down. That's the kind of thing I like!

I try to give my characters some of that same quirkiness. One of the best compliments I ever received was from someone who said that my books were "never satisfied with being merely cute."

Q: Before TOON Books came along, had you already turned back to making comics?

A: Yes. Seven or eight years ago, I got to the point where I was fed up with my picture book career. So I stopped cold and I said to myself, "I am just going to draw and write whatever I like, without any thought of publication." I wrote several stories that I had wanted to write for some time. At least half of these were comics stories, so I was moving in that direction. Then one day I was talking to my agent and said, "Well, maybe I'll do comics for beginning readers. It has never been done before, and somebody's got to do it!" I thought maybe I was the right person for the job.

A few months later, I got a call from Françoise Mouly, who was just starting TOON Books. It was great to realize we were both thinking along the same lines. She and her husband, Art Spiegelman, had read some of the little Patrick books, which I had done as picture books in the 1980s, to their own children. They weren't comics, but they had word balloons and Art had remembered them. Françoise probably found me on Google.

Q: Had the publication of Art Spiegelman's *Maus* been a big event for you?

A: Not particularly, because by then I had drifted away from comics. I saw it and admired it—at a time when there were so few comics. Certainly, I was very aware of it and intrigued by what Art had done.

Q: Why has there been such an explosion of creativity in the graphic novel realm?

A: It has to do with the visual age in which we're living. With computers everywhere, ours is becoming a more and more visual age. So I don't think it's a fad and [feel] that comics will be around for quite a while.

Q: Why are comics a good format for beginning readers?

A: I find that comics are easy to reread. I tend to reread the comics I love more than I would reread a novel. There is something about the format that makes you want to go back and follow it again and again through the pictures.

Q: Is it the thought that you might have missed something the first time?

A: Sometimes it's that. Just recently all the Donald Duck books by Carl Barks have been reprinted and I have been rereading them. The thing I find amazing about them is that it's almost impossible to just look at the art. I've tried and you just can't do it. You have to read the text. It's so beautifully synchronized. It's a mystery to me how he did that. Of all the comics I know, his are the most readable; there is such a total integration of the pictures and text.

Also, there are all sorts of fun things you can do educationally in comics. If there is an unusual word that I want to keep in the text, I'll find a way to do a little picture or icon and put it in a thought bubble. I did that in *The Toy Breaker* where Penny is talking about treasure, and I added an icon in a thought bubble of a treasure chest. That's something you cannot do in any other genre.

Q: Tell me more about how comics "work."

A: Well, there is the pacing—the way the panels are divided. In *Benny and Penny in Just Pretend,* in the part where they fall down the hill, the panels are all skewed and going at crazy angles. Or if I'm drawing a claustrophobic scene, the panels may suddenly narrow or be smaller than usual to emphasize that feeling.

Q: Sometimes you'll have a picture in a frame, and the image next to it might not be in a frame. Why is that?

A: Sometimes it is just to add variety. Most of those choices are intuitive. I'll look at a picture, and I'll see it without a border or with one. Sometimes I'll do a panel that has a very thick border or a double border. It just feels right. When I first got into children's books, I spent hours and hours obsessing about composition. Now it has become second nature.

Q: You mentioned wanting to be an actor when you were very young. Your characters look like they're acting on the page. Do you think of them that way?

A: Animators have sometimes described themselves as actors with a pencil. That's probably true. As I've gotten older, I've gotten better at expressions and body language. I spend a lot of time drawing the characters to get their expressions right. Benny and Penny are pretty simple, and so there is a tendency to put them in similar poses again and again. So I'm always trying to find a new pose that is less common and more expressive and truer to their characters. I just did a drawing of Benny running in which his right arm is pushed forward in the way that athletes do. It adds some variety to the illustrations. Animators talk about a character being "off-model," which means that the character does not look exactly like he should.

Sometimes I'll see that I've done that with Benny and Penny. But even we human beings don't always look the same in every picture that's taken of us. I have one drawing of Benny in which his expression reminds me of the actor David Duchovny. I don't know why! That's just something I see. Probably no one else will notice it. I don't see myself, particularly, in my illustrations, though other people may see me in my characters—maybe in my character Patrick most of all.

Q: Do you think — and see — like an artist all the time?

A: When I open a book by another artist, I'll sometimes sense that the layout is chaotic or doesn't make sense. If I'm watching a movie, I may be impressed by a certain shot that stands out as unusual. I'll take a walk and look at the trees, and sometimes I will see something that I think I can incorporate into one of my drawings. But I don't walk around with a sketchbook, and I do very little research. I remember what I see. What fascinates me about drawing is seeing what comes out of my unconscious. Google Images has been a great help for when I have had to draw a particular kind of bird. But when I look at a tree, I realize there's no way I could ever duplicate nature, which is so beautiful and perfect, so I don't even try. Instead, I sit down and get started, and whatever comes out is the way I draw the tree.

Q: Tell me about "Mister Bear Makes His Move." Why did you want to tell that story?

A: When I saw that the topic you chose for each artist was "the city," I laughed because I'd been trying to leave the big city for years—first San Francisco, then New York. While I still love big cities, I no longer care to live in them. I'd been seeking a small city and felt I'd found the perfect one in Asheville, North Carolina. However, when I

The basics are all here, but compare these finely detailed sketches with the finishes on pages 28–29, and you will observe many small touches and tweaks that sharpen both the humor and the design.

moved, I spent the first several weeks not in Asheville itself but at my friends' retreat center in Black Mountain, forty-five minutes away by car—150 acres and not a Starbucks in sight! Just trees, bugs, a noisy creek, and *cold,* lots of cold! It didn't help that I took a nasty spill down some wet wooden steps shortly after arriving!

I found myself considering if there was still a possibility that I could change my plans and hightail it back to NYC. (There wasn't.) I wrote this little two-pager in a small office off the barn in about twenty minutes.

But most children's stories have happy endings. Once I left the mountain and became a resident of the city of Asheville, my misgivings vanished. I can't imagine living anywhere else. All those big-city travails are but a memory.

Q: Do you have a work routine?

A: In the past, when I was writing more, I would start out by writing gobbledygook—sheer nonsense. I found that very quickly it would evolve into regular writing. But I don't do that anymore.

I find that the different phases of making a book each have their own climate. When I am just coming up with an idea for a book, it's a chaotic time, with a lot of nervous tension, and I'm not able to work long hours. I have to put the ideas down, then leave them alone, maybe go for a walk or go to the grocery store, and let things gestate. By the time I am ready to do the dummy or layout for the book, things are a little different, not so tense. The real crunch comes when I do the final art. That's when I will work ten or twelve hours a day to get the book done. But not at the beginning!

Q: Do you revise your work?

A: Constantly! Especially the art. I just changed the order of panels in the book I'm working on now and the order of the text. I haven't told my editor yet! It's all for the sake of clarity. I change things right up until the end.

Q: Do you hear from readers about your books?

A: I was at one school in Illinois where the kids wanted me to draw Benny and Penny's mother. As I drew her, I would ask for help with questions like "What kind of dress should she have?" They kept piling on the makeup and the clothes, and by the time I was done, [Benny and] Penny's mother looked like a whore! I love the spontaneity of kids. One little boy, a kindergartner or maybe even a preschooler, asked, "How do you do the cover?" I replied, rather earnestly, "Well, first you do a layout, and then you worry about the type . . ." I was going on and on until he interrupted me and said, "No. How do you make the cover so stiff?" He thought I actually made the covers myself, one by one, from scratch.

Q: You seem to enjoy making books for readers like him.

A: It's odd. I don't know why this is, but I somehow have the ability to capture the lingo of preschoolers. I don't remember much about my toddler and preschool years. My own earliest memories go back to when I was seven or eight. But I have a facility for nailing the way young kids speak.

Q: How has your art changed over the years?

A: The world of children's literature has changed. When I began my career, it simply wasn't possible to include dark stuff in my books. But I can now. The graphic novel I've been working on for years—and which is finally coming to fruition—has a lot of dark elements. And it's telling that my favorite living graphic artist is Mike Mignola. (I love the bimonthly comic *Mouse Guard* too, so I haven't totally gone over to the dark side!)

Q: What do you like best about making books?

A: When I'm writing my books, my thought is always about clarity: on finding the most direct way of saying something. Everything in my books—the placement, the characters, the expressions on the characters' faces, the way the panels are composed—is there to further the communication. For me, art is all about communication. If anything, I would like to think that I'm a good communicator.

KAZU KIBUISHI
(Born 1978, Tokyo, Japan)

I believe a lot in focusing on just a few things," Kazu Kibuishi told an interviewer in 2013, soon after he had been chosen to design new cover art for the hugely popular Harry Potter series. Kibuishi told reporters at the time that he had accepted the plum assignment after a brief bout of uncertainty: up until then, after all, he had concentrated almost all his creative energies on just *two* related passions: comics and animation.

Kibuishi was still a child when he and his mother and brother moved to the United States from Japan. He arrived in California filled with vivid images of Japanese TV robot action heroes like Ultraman. In college he majored in animation and drew a comic strip called *Clive and Cabbage* for the student newspaper. Then, after working for a time in an animation studio on commercials and games, he opted for the greater freedom—and risk—of going it alone as a freelance artist.

Kibuishi proved to be highly adept at marketing his work. He launched his adventure strip *Copper* in 2002 by posting installments on the Web, and in 2004 created *Flight,* a comics annual, as a showcase for himself and his friends. In 2012 he added the Explorer series, to the delight of his growing fan base.

Kibuishi's most ambitious project to date has been the long-running Amulet series of graphic novels, which take place within a mythic realm that he continues to elaborate on and explore. "Every time I do a new book," he reports, "I feel like I'm on a new adventure. . . . I just fall into the story. I let the characters take me somewhere."

Amulet stories are inventive, fast paced, and as easy to follow as the stories Kibuishi always favored as a child "I like to tell parents and teachers," he once said, "that classic literature is simply popular entertainment that was popular a long time ago. And kids who are reluctant readers are simply readers who haven't found a story that engages them." Kibuishi's storytelling may flow effortlessly, but his luminous artwork is so painstakingly drawn that fellow comics artist and theorist Scott McCloud once remarked in admiration, "It hurts my hands when I look at it." Kibuishi now has a studio of his own—Bolt City Productions—where on any given day an app or other media project is as likely to be in the works as a book. As Kibuishi told an interviewer, "I actually have people"—a staff of artists—creating some of the illustrations for his books. "Can you make those backgrounds look better?" He seems rather amazed to have arrived at this point. "I'm the guy," he says, "who draws less and less." We spoke by phone on February 25, 2014.

• •

Leonard S. Marcus: What were you like as a child?

Kazu Kibuishi: A friendly guy. I wasn't a social butterfly, but I didn't shy away from hanging out with other people. I was a good student when I wanted to be. I was one of the best students in the second half of high school, though not in the first. I got my grades up as soon as I realized I would have to if I wanted to get into a good film school.

I was always into sports. For a long time as a kid, I thought about playing professional baseball. Of course, I don't know if I actually would have cut it. I played shortstop because that is the position from which you command the field. I liked being in the right place to tell everybody what might be coming next. I would play out every scenario in my mind in advance, so that the minute the ball came off the bat, I knew what was supposed to happen.

It's exactly the same way for me with my work with comics. With Amulet, people are shocked to see that I do most of the drawing for a book in the last couple of months. I spend most of the time going over all the possible scenarios in my mind beforehand—before I ever put a word or line on paper. Eventually I decide, "*This* path is probably the smartest one. This will most likely yield the best result." Once I make that basic decision, I draw the book incredibly fast.

Q: What comics did you love growing up?

A: As a child, *Garfield* was the comic I always looked to. I wanted to *be* Jim Davis when I was five or six. I read *Calvin and Hobbes* in high school. Also, *Mad* magazine. *Mad*'s Mort Drucker was another one of my heroes.

Q: Did you grow up bilingual?

A: I came to the U.S. when I was three. I still understand Japanese and can speak Japanese without an accent. But my vocabulary is that of a three-year-old!

Q: Do you feel a kinship with the Japanese comics tradition?

A: Not really. I didn't grow up on Japanese comics outside of the manga that my grandmother kept on the shelves of her Japanese restaurant in California for the businessmen who would come and have lunch. They weren't made for kids, but I would look at them now and then, although I couldn't read them.

Q: What about Erik Larsen?

A: I was a fan of *Savage Dragon* and of all his *Spider-Man* issues. He was a childhood hero of mine, too. So it was a thrill when I later met him at the Alternative Press Expo in California, where he unexpectedly came up to the exhibit table of my friends and me and said, "I want to publish *Flight*"—the first comics collection I edited, with original stories that my friends and I had done.

Q: When did you first see yourself as an artist and a writer?

A: It started with an interest in drawing for Marvel or DC. A high school friend and I would spend our after-school hours drawing late into the night, pretty much every day, and all through the summer. We had this notion to become professional comics artists. Then one day I visited one of the studios where these comics were being published, and I realized I didn't like the stories they were producing, and that I wouldn't want to draw them. I saw myself as very much a writer at the time and was writing poems and short stories for my friends as well as for the high school literary journal. So I decided this wouldn't be a career for me. I thought, "All right, then I'll be a screenwriter," and so I enrolled in the film studies program at the University of California at Santa Barbara.

My mom had drilled it into my head as a child that I was going to be a doctor, and I had pretty much resigned myself to the idea early on. My vision of my future was that I might draw caricatures of my patients and hang them on my waiting room wall. I thought how horrible that would be. It was like a fever-dream nightmare! I started to draw more and more, out of fear that it was my last chance. By the time I was a teenager, I thought, "I better get it all out now because I am not going to be able to do this later." In a strange way, that fear is what eventually drove me into drawing for a living: the fear that I would otherwise have to do something else for the rest of my life.

At the same time, I kept looking for a path that would allow me to continue drawing. After deciding that working for Marvel or DC was not the right choice for me, I began to believe that filmmaking might be a serious vocation, work that would allow me to put my skills to good use.

Q: What led you back to comics?

A: While I was in college, I drew a daily comic for the school news-paper. The deadlines were really tight, and I learned to work like a professional. And I ended up producing a tremendous amount of content that I was able to carry away with me after school. I wasn't sure what my film degree qualified me for, but my comic strip helped me get jobs as a graphic designer and as an illustrator for magazines.

Q: It sounds like you were open to trying lots of different things.

A: For a time I worked as a graphic designer at an architectural firm. It was the wrong job for me in every possible way. I completely shut down and actually ended up having a nervous breakdown. After that, while I was living at home with my parents for a while, I started my comic strip *Copper,* which is about an adventurous boy and his fearful dog. I was able to explore some philosophical ideas that interested me, and it was a good chance for me to work some stuff out. Initially, I drew *Copper* for a magazine that no longer exists called *Yoke,* and it was unpaid work. I later serialized it myself on my website, and that is when it took on a life of its own. Scott McCloud and Jeff Smith—two of my heroes—found it there and reached out to me. They told me my work was great and that I should continue

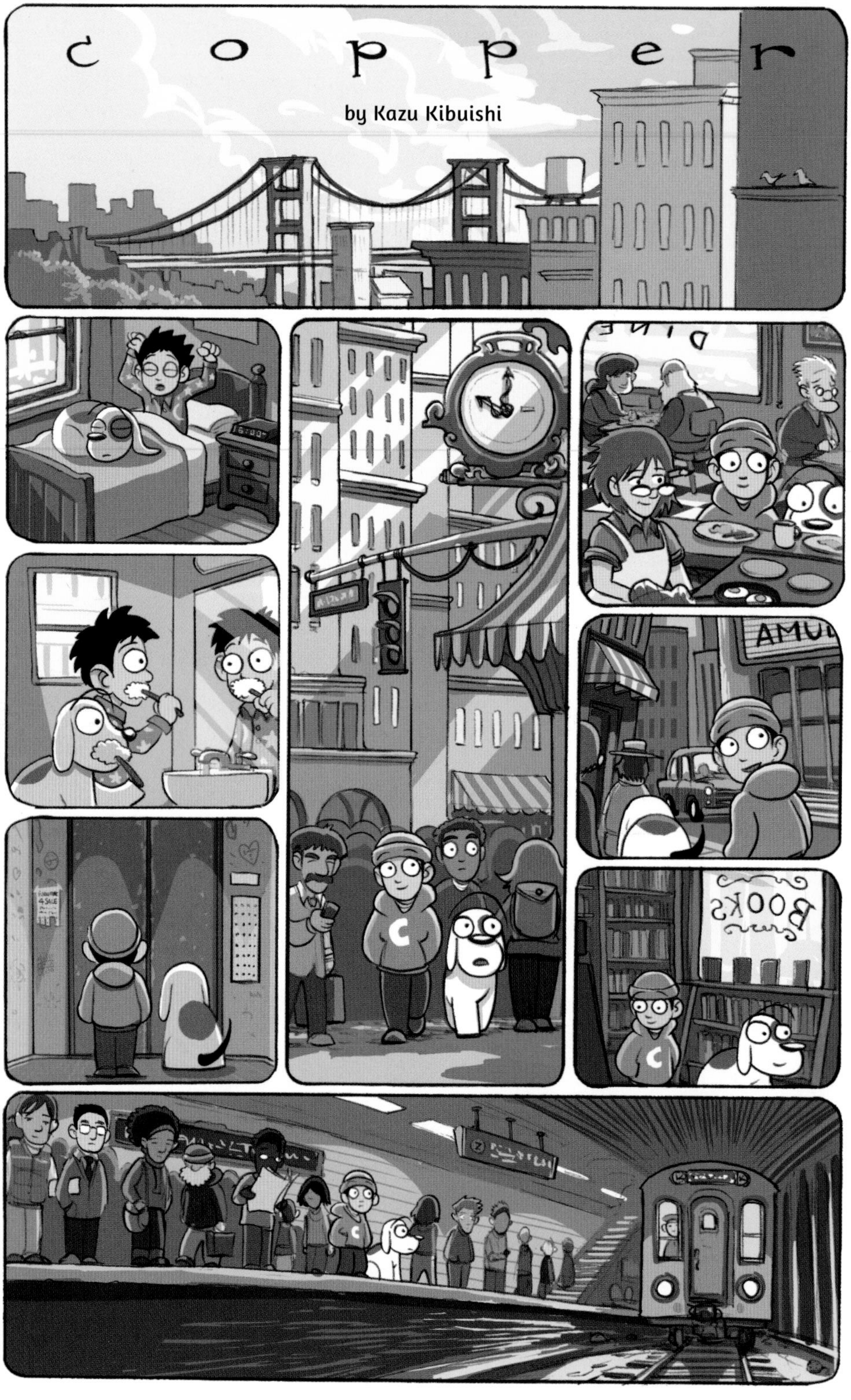
copper
by Kazu Kibuishi

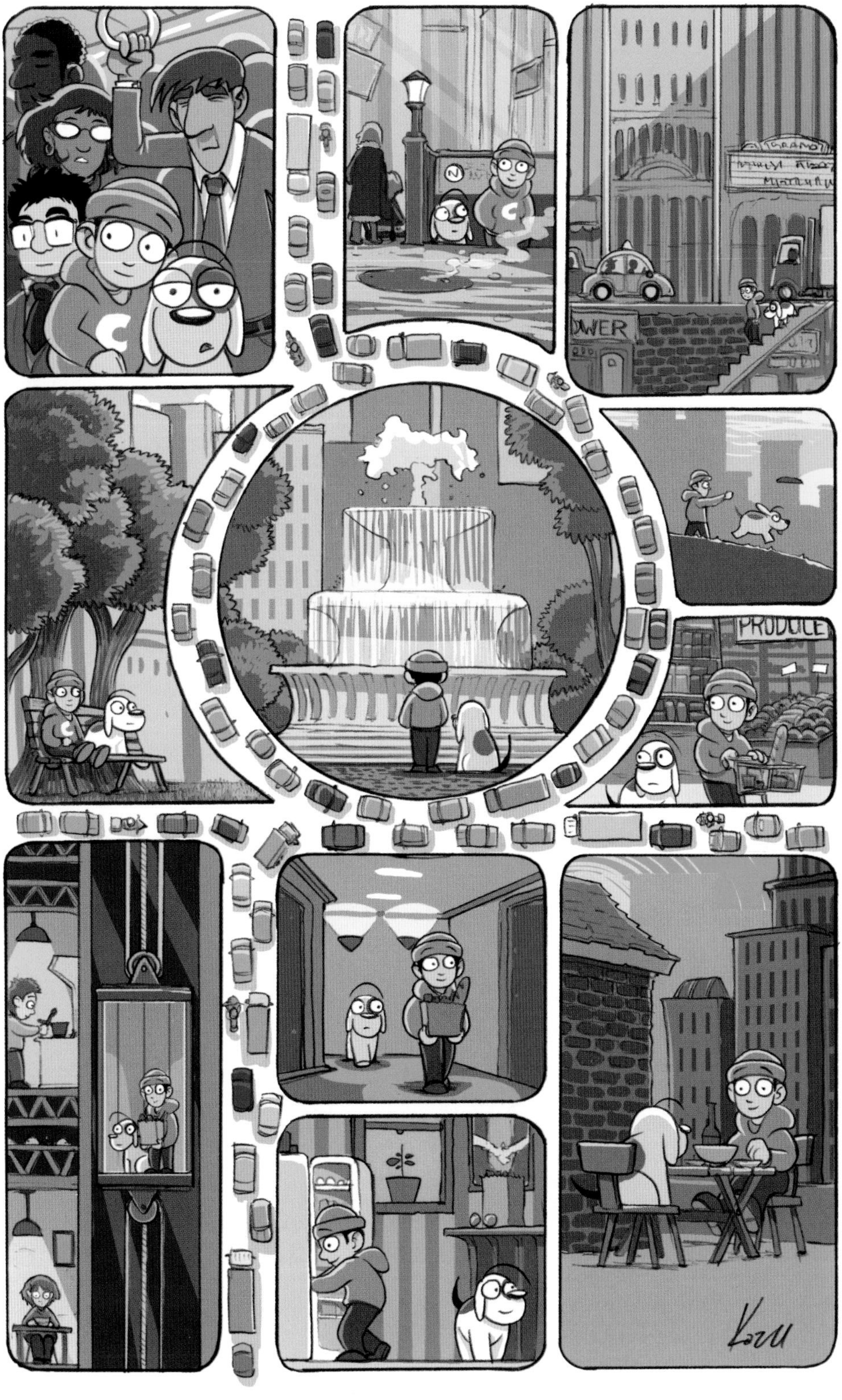
PRODUCE

doing it. I was working at an animation studio and drawing *Copper* in my free time. Eventually I was able to spend all my time doing comics.

Q: How did you get involved with web comics?

A: When I was starting, Scott McCloud had a group of web comics artist disciples. I thought that one of them, Derek Kirk Kim, was drawing the best comics anywhere. At the time people thought that web comics were amateurish—that a comic *had* to be published in order for it to be a serious piece of work. It was really just a snobbish thing, in the same way that for a long time people thought that film was automatically better than television. But seeing Derek's work on the Web changed all that for me, and he inspired me to create my own website and to post *Copper* there.

After college the Web gave me the ability to create my own newspaper. I designed my site to *look* like a newspaper. At that point I was almost addicted to drawing comics. I needed to do it, and it didn't matter if I was being paid to do it or not.

Q: How do you see film in relation to comics?

A: I worked in film animation for a time and enjoyed it. But I came to feel that there was a glut of talent in the film industry. It seemed that a lot of very talented film people were just waiting in line, and that many of them would probably never have the opportunity to show off their stuff. I felt, "I'm really not needed here"—and it started to dawn on me that it was a better idea for me to go someplace that needed me a little bit more. When I looked at the comics world, it was kind of a sad story. I thought, "I used to love this place, and look at it now." There wasn't much out there besides Jeff Smith. I followed Jeff in on the same path. I wanted to be part of what I thought of as a rebuilding process for comics.

One of my goals has been to introduce comics to young readers and create a love for comics at an early age. That's one of the big reasons I got into doing comics for kids, even though some of my friends thought that kids' comics were not "serious" work. They *can* be serious, of course! And that is what led me to start Amulet. I was twenty-four or twenty-five at the time and didn't have any kids yet. So it was really difficult for me at first to get into the right mind-set.

Q: Would you want the Amulet series to become a film?

A: Most definitely! It was always meant to become a movie or series of films. My hope is that the movies and the books will coexist well, in much the way that that is true for Harry Potter. I think everyone involved with Harry Potter took good care of the mythology. I would not want the movies to stamp out the books.

With the big Hollywood superhero movies, most people don't even realize that the stories started out on the printed page. The comic book artists and writers who created them are almost never mentioned. On a recent trip to Cleveland, I decided to visit the various local sites of historical importance to comics. I drove to the house where Jerry Siegel and Joe Shuster wrote the first *Superman* comics, for instance. It's just a guy's house, with a plaque outside. But the owner invited me in and showed me his collection of Superman bobbleheads. He showed me his Superman Room!

Q: How do you feel about turning the "classics" into graphic novel form?

A: I would love to do a graphic novel of H. G. Wells's *The Time Machine*. Ironically, with all the work it takes to keep the Amulet series going, I don't know when I'll have the time to do it. *A Wizard of Earthsea* by Ursula K. Le Guin is another classic I would love to do. One reason

High-tech master though he is, when Kazu Kibuishi starts work on a comic, he likes to do his preliminary thinking with a blue pencil in hand.

for my interest in doing so is that *A Wizard of Earthsea* is a hard book to read, and I think that a graphic novelization of it might help the audience it was intended for.

Q: Tell me about the comic you created for this book, "Copper." It looks back, in a way, to your beginnings in comics.

A: When I hear the word "city," I immediately think of New York City first, so I chose to depict life in New York in this comic. I was born in

This elegant hand-dawn line art is ready for the addition of digital color.

Tokyo, grew up in Los Angeles, and have traveled all over the world. So I've always been familiar with big cities, but nothing really compares with New York. The comic is a little tribute to my friends in the publishing industry, most of whom live in or near Manhattan, and I loved getting another chance to draw my characters Copper and Fred. My focus has been on Amulet for several years now, and I've rarely had the opportunity to draw these guys, so this was a great chance for me to spend a little time with some imaginary friends as a tribute to my friends in real life.

Q: Do you find some things hard to draw?

A: As long as I know what a thing looks like, it's not hard for me to draw it. I have a bunch of shorthand techniques that allow me to mold things I'm very comfortable drawing to look like things I've never drawn before, based on their shape and volume and form and viscosity. I guess I think like a 3-D animator. I build a drawing like someone building with LEGOs. I carry a sketchbook everywhere I go and draw so much that it's really not hard anymore. It's like shooting free throws for a basketball player.

Q: Why do comics artists so often band together as friends?

A: Because making comics is still an outsider's profession. Often the artist's family is disapproving. They'll say, "This person is not going to do well in life!" So you're bonded by the idea that you're bound to be a failure before you start. This has changed quite a bit for the better in the last few years. Still, the superstars who make a tremendous living as comics artists only come along once or twice in a generation.

Q: Do you hear from your readers?

A: I was just in San Antonio with thousands of kids who are big fans of Amulet. Events like that one get bigger and bigger each year. When I first started, maybe one person would show up! I feel a great responsibility to them. My job is to give them the best book possible. There's Amulet fan fiction now. Some kids are starting to put my characters in relationships I never intended.

Q: What is the most satisfying thing about doing your books?

A: I don't know if I can point to just one thing. Every time I make an Amulet book, it's as though I am getting to direct a big-budget movie, but without having to spend all that money to do it. It all just comes from my brain, I get it down on paper, and then a ten-year-old can see pretty clearly what I am trying to do. That's an amazing experience. Being able to share a vision with somebody is very exciting in any field.

Then there is the interactivity I have with all the teachers, librarians, and students. I think of myself as a worldwide teacher's aide. By creating books that kids like to read and by visiting with schoolchildren, I am in a sense making it easier for teachers to do their jobs. And I love knowing other comic book artists, who are some of the best people I've ever met. Being part of that community is fantastic.

One more good thing about what I do is that because I work at home, I am able to be with my family all the time and to watch my kids grow up every day. I don't know too many people who get to see their kids so much of the time. That's a huge, huge thing—for me anyway.

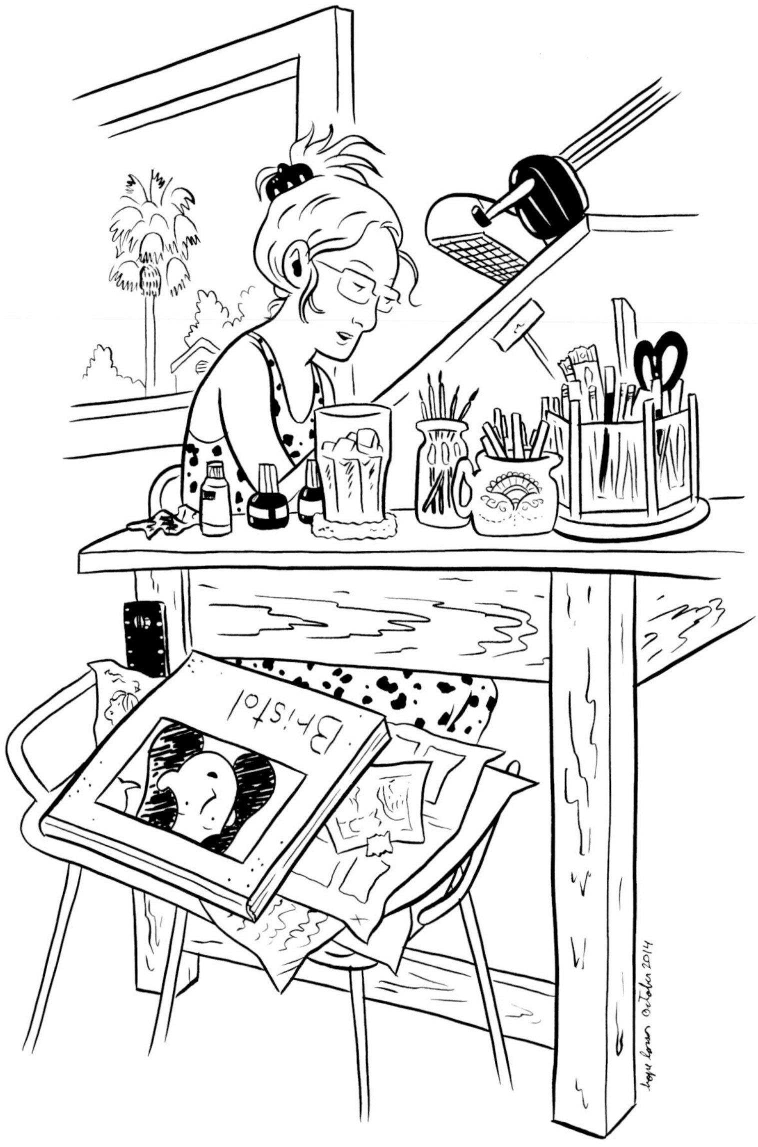
Bristol
hope larson October 2014

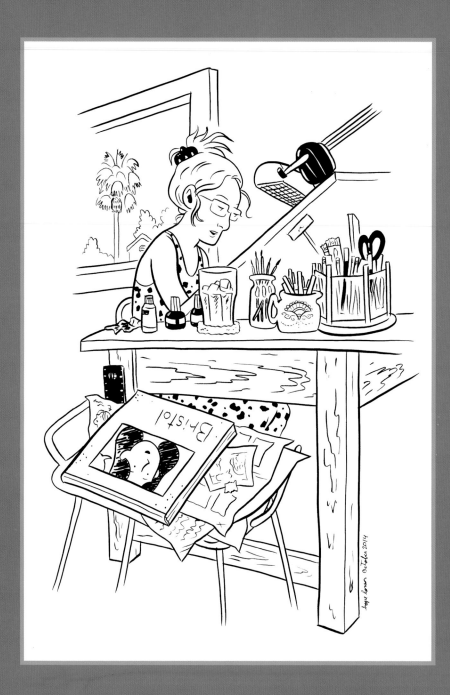

HOPE LARSON

(Born 1982, Asheville, North Carolina)

When Hope Larson was a girl, superhero comics were everywhere, and most were clearly aimed at boy readers. Not surprisingly, she looked elsewhere for the stories she craved: to classic fantasy fiction like C. S. Lewis's Chronicles of Narnia and Madeleine L'Engle's *A Wrinkle in Time,* and to the stories she herself was always writing. The world of comics first caught her eye during a year her family spent in France, where she fell in love with the illustrated adventures of Tintin and Astérix, and with other comics that were unlike any she had seen back home. As she came of age artistically, she turned to the comics format for her own stories as well and found it was equally well suited for tales based on history (a favorite subject of hers) and the everyday lives of girls like the one she had been.

Larson's creative life came full circle when a publisher e-mailed her out of the blue with an invitation to create a graphic novel based on *A Wrinkle in Time.* Meg Murry—the story's gawky, misunderstood, courageous young heroine—had always been such a favorite character of hers that Larson had reread L'Engle's book often as a teenager. She knew that adapting *Wrinkle* would be an epic undertaking, not least because the original novel was itself quite long. (Larson would later recall that it had taken her a month just to draw all the speech balloons.) Of even greater concern was the fear that it might be impossible to satisfy L'Engle's legions of die-hard fans. Her worries proved unwarranted; *A Wrinkle in Time: The Graphic Novel* became a best-seller and won Larson her second Will Eisner Award. Then it was time for a break. "I went to ice cream school," she told a reporter, "which is actually quite science-heavy; Dr. Kate Murry would approve."

Larson was at home in Los Angeles when we recorded this conversation by phone on November 15, 2013.

• •

Leonard S. Marcus: What were you like as a child?

Hope Larson: I was always drawing. Writing too. One of my earlier memories is of dictating a story to my dad and him typing it up. Then I drew illustrations on the pages when he was done. Even in second grade, I would do illustrated books that were stapled together. A lot of them were about unicorns! Typical little-girl stuff. I was always working with illustrated stories.

We were living in Asheville, North Carolina, which is not a big city, and our house had a big backyard with a creek in it and lots of trees and a stand of bamboo. I would spend all of my time out there. My parents also owned a chunk of land in the nearby countryside. We would go out there on a regular basis and hike in the woods.

Q: What were you reading then?

A: A lot of fantasy. The first books I remember reading are C. S. Lewis's The Chronicles of Narnia, which my parents introduced me to, and Lloyd Alexander's The Chronicles of Prydain. From there I got into Tolkien.

Q: Were your parents involved in the arts?

A: No. My mom's a nurse, and my dad is an economics professor. My brother grew up to become a computer programmer. So as an artist and writer, I'm the odd one out in my immediate family. But my maternal grandfather was an artist and a sign painter and print-maker. He was an artist jack-of-all-trades. He died before I was born, but I feel that everything I have artistically has come from him.

Q: You seem to like drawing trees.

A: I do. It's hard to mess them up, and you don't have to break out a ruler. Straight lines are such a pain! I find it relaxing to draw trees. If I'm drawing a forest scene, I start with just one tree and build around it. I start with an orderly image and go from there.

Q: You spent a year of your childhood in France.

A: I was seven going on eight and didn't know any French when I got there. My dad was on sabbatical and was translating a book from French to English. I think he used that project as an excuse for us to live in France for a year. It was an amazing experience. They put my brother and me in the village school with all the French kids, and we learned by total immersion. That is where I read my first comics: *Tintin, Astérix,* and *My Little Pony* comics, which came out once a week, and *Scrooge McDuck,* which was huge in France.

When I came back to the United States, it was hard to find that kind of thing. There were just a lot of superhero comics. I wasn't into them, and I could tell my mom didn't especially approve of them. So from about age eight or nine through high school, I didn't read any comics. Then I got into manga and from there into indie comics.

Q: Did you get interested in superhero comics later on?

A: No, and I am still not into them. I don't like the way most of them look stylistically. Because I didn't grow up with the rhythm of serialized storytelling, it's hard for me to get into it now. In the few superhero comics I've read, it seems that a lot of time has been devoted to catching people up to what has already happened in the story. There's just not much there that appeals to me.

Q: What was the appeal of manga to you?

A: The first thing that got my attention was the art. I thought it was the most beautiful thing I had ever seen. The first one I read was *Ranma ½*, by Rumiko Takahashi, who I think is one of the richest women in Japan! She is an extremely successful, extremely talented manga artist. A lot of what she does is for boys, but they're really lighthearted and fun and slapsticky and action packed. I was so into all that.

Q: What about indie comics? What did you see in them?

A: They were a little edgier. As I was moving into college, I was looking for cooler, edgier things. Daniel Clowes's *Ghost World* was a hugely important book for me and still is.

Q: In college you studied animation.

A: I studied film for a year and had a little bit of training both in live-action moviemaking and animation. I did life drawing on the side because I thought I might go into animation. But I ended up not clicking with film and decided to concentrate instead on illustration, printmaking, and painting.

Q: How would you compare the graphic novel with film as art forms?

A: I would say that the big similarity is in the editing. In a comic you are telling a story by putting different images together to create a sequence. Editing a film is essentially the same process. You have all this footage and you think, "OK, this moment and this image are going to work well next to that moment and that image." It's all about transitions. That is the one big similarity. When I started making comics after having had some experience editing films, I immediately thought, "I know how to do this." But the differences between comics and film are huge. Making comics is a very solitary art form whereas filmmaking is a very social art form.

Q: Your book *Mercury* is in part a story about gold miners in 1800s Canada. Have you always been interested in history? In doing historical research?

A: Growing up, I liked to read about the American Revolution, and, yes, I love research. It's easier for me to make up a story by starting with something real that I can build on, rather than building up fantasy from nothing.

Q: How did you research *Mercury*?

A: The story is set in Nova Scotia, where I was living at the time. I had access to the archives in Halifax, and I found a book of local myths from which I pulled various details. I went through genealogy books in which I would sometimes find interesting brief biographies of individuals from which I took other details.

Q: Why are there so many good Canadian graphic novelists, including your former husband, Bryan Lee O'Malley, and Seth?

A: I think it's partly because Canada has some really good comics shops that nurture young talent. If you have access to a wide range of art to inspire you, and you have people who are going to be excited to sell your first zine or mini-comic, then you're more likely to stick with it and get serious about it. Toronto and Montreal, especially, have a ton of cartoonists living there.

Q: Comics artists seem to enjoy being part of a community.

A: Totally. We're spread out across the United States and the world, and are all working at the same solitary pursuit, so we have found that it is good to reach out for support to other people who are doing the same thing. We're all on Twitter all day long! You do some drawing, and then you check in with all of your friends who are also working on comics and talking about comics and art and writing. I think it helps us all to keep from going crazy! The other big topic is always tendonitis and exercises for your hand or wrist.

Q: How did all this start?

A: Web comics were out there, and most of us came out of that. Lots of manga were being translated from Japanese into English and flooding the market. Barnes & Noble had a huge manga section, and you'd go in there and see kids sitting all over the floor, reading those books. Manga series run to ten, twenty, even thirty volumes long. It must have interested publishers to see kids buying so many of those books.

Then in 2005 book publishers started expressing interest in graphic novels. Suddenly, publishers were snapping people up right and left, and it seemed that everybody had a book deal—and were finally getting paid enough money to just sit down and focus and do a book and get it done and get it out. Then in 2008, when the economy went kaput, things got difficult for a few years. But now we're starting to hit our stride. A lot of great books that have been in the works for years are coming out, and publishers are starting to figure out how to sell the books and get them to their audience. I think that my peers and I, who were starting out around 2005, are now coming into our own as artists. I've done a lot of books at this point, but I still feel that I am kind of just starting out and putting all the pieces together. It's a daunting thing to do a graphic novel. You have to be able to draw it *and* write it. It takes a while to get up to speed. I think that that is what is happening now and that we are all finding our own voices.

Q: Did you think about who your audience was?

A: At first I didn't think I was writing for anyone in particular. I thought, "These are the stories I feel like writing." Then when I sold *Chiggers,* it dawned on me that I was basically going to be a young adult cartoonist because that is what they were selling me as. So I had to make a conscious decision to tell those kinds of stories in the future. That's what they wanted from me, and that is what I felt was most natural anyway.

Q: Do you see yourself in any of your stories?

A: *Chiggers* is probably the closest to being an autobiographical story, but even that one isn't *very* autobiographical. One reason I turned to writing historical fiction, in fact, was to make it clear that the stories are not just about me.

Q: In *Chiggers* you give instructions for making a friendship bracelet. Do you think of making your books in a similar way, as a kind of handicraft for your readers to try one day?

A: Probably. I haven't thought about that. In my new book *Who Is AC?*

STARLAND

by Hope Larson

I saw him in Griffith Park, in the middle of the city, right by the Trails Cafe.

At first, I thought he was homeless.

Then I thought he was an actor. Something cooked up by the studios. But I couldn't find the camera, and no one came to make me sign a waiver.

It was the coyote that convinced me.

They both had the same wild eyes.

I didn't even try to take his picture. I mean, you've seen E.T., right?

The part with the plastic sheeting, and the guys in clean suits?

It would've been like—

Wait!

But he didn't.

After that, I went back every day. I did homework while I waited.

My G.P.A. went up half a point. That's how bad I wanted to see him.

I never did.

A year later, a star fell in the park.

The whole town saw the flash.

When they eventually found the crater, the meteorite was gone.

the main character makes little chapbook zines. That is definitely a nod to the time when I was just starting out—a time I look back on very fondly, when I could draw a comic, bring it to the copy shop, and give out copies to friends, sometimes all in the same day.

Q: Had you known *A Wrinkle in Time* as a child?

A: Yes. It was another of those important books for me growing up. I read it and the rest of the Time Quintet, and I remember that the bookstore I went to as a kid had an entire shelf devoted to Madeleine L'Engle, and I knew that if I went to the store and got something from that shelf, it was going to be really good. Over the years I have reread the Time Quintet books many times.

When I received an e-mail asking if I would want to do a graphic novel version of *A Wrinkle in Time,* I couldn't believe my luck. I thought at first that it must be a mistake or somebody's idea of a joke.

Q: Given its power as a story and its special value for so many readers, how did you go about imagining and planning your own version of *A Wrinkle in Time*? What did you do first?

A: I sat down with the book, which I hadn't reread for a couple of years, and I wrote the script as I was rereading it. One reason that I thought *A Wrinkle in Time* was a good candidate for being made into a graphic novel was that there is not all that much description in it. That meant that I had many opportunities to play visually and fill in the blanks. Madeleine L'Engle's text is almost all dialogue, and nearly all of the original dialogue is in the graphic novel too.

It went through remarkably few stages and revisions. I couldn't figure out a way to cut the story, and I didn't want to anyway. Very little changed from my sketches to the finished art. I used blue as an extra color because it felt right and because much of the story takes place at night or in dark places, so it seemed a good choice. Also, blue tends to recede in space, rather than pop out at you. Red is a very aggressive color, so I did not want red, and my editor was very adamant that I not use purple. I don't know why!

I had to think carefully about how to draw Meg because my visual image of her was very different from the way she is actually described in the book. She goes through the story with a black eye, for instance, and I had forgotten all about that. For clothes and hairstyles and other details of that kind, I used a 1962 Sears and Roebuck catalog that I found on eBay.

Q: How do you think of the graphic novel version of a book, especially of a classic like *A Wrinkle in Time,* in relation to the original?

A: I see it as being supplementary and as an homage. It's certainly not in any sense a replacement for the original. My hope is always that kids who read the graphic novel first will go on to read the novel.

Q: What inspired you to create "Starland"?

A: This comic is about my love of Los Angeles. It's a big city, but it's not a city in the way that New York or Chicago or Toronto is a city. It's spread out, and it's full of unexpected pockets of wilderness. There's Griffith Park, where this story takes place, a 4,000-acre park full of hiking trails and wildlife like coyotes and cougars. There are also a number of smaller but still sizable parks, including Elysian Park (600 acres) and Debs Park (282 acres). In spite of the cars and the smog, nature is a big part of life in Los Angeles. The other aspect of LA that I wanted to touch on is the fact that many people here lead hidden lives. Everyone's either trying to blend in and go incognito, or they're fronting like they're somebody important when they don't even know where next month's rent is coming from. So, it was fun

Like a tightrope walker working without a net, Hope Larson made only one set of preliminary drawings before completing "Starland" as digital art.

to write a story about this character in Griffith Park who couldn't possibly be what he appears to be, but is.

Q: Do you have a daily work routine?

A: I do. When I'm writing, I get up at seven every day, and I write from eight or nine in the morning until noon. Then I take a break and maybe go for a run. Around two, I go out to a coffee shop and work there for two or three more hours. Then I'm done for the day. When I'm drawing, my schedule is similar except that I will have a page count that I need to hit, whereas for writing it is much harder

to set a specific goal. By the time I start drawing, the script is already in place, and I know that I just have to sit down and draw. If I'm drawing "pencils," I will want to have finished four by the end of the day; if I'm doing "inks," I will do two per day. Inking is a purely mechanical process. I listen to a lot of audiobooks at that stage!

Q: What are some of the things you like best about making comics?

A: I like telling stories that have the feel of a novel: stories that are big and all of a piece. And I feel like there should be more stories out there for girls, and I try to tell them.

DANICA
NOVGORODOFF
(Born 1980, Louisville, Kentucky)

DCor Marvel?' To many comics fans," Danica Novgorodoff once observed, only half kidding, "this question is as fundamental as 'Chocolate or vanilla?' 'Yankees or Red Sox?' 'Boxers or briefs?'" Novgorodoff's own response is a characteristically surprising one. She claims never to have read a single comic book from either of the industry's two publishing giants. As a graphic novelist, she says, she has looked instead to a wide variety of other sources for heroes and role models: the gods of Greek mythology; filmmakers Alfred Hitchcock and Werner Herzog; Japanese poets and Mexican folk artists; and the horse trainers and firefighters she has known, among others. Novgorodoff's graphic novels are as unexpected as her inspirations. This is as true of the "camera angles" from which she draws a scene as it is of the stories she tells.

Soft-spoken and outwardly modest, Novgorodoff runs marathons, rides horses, is a fearless traveler, and keeps to a highly disciplined work routine. She prefers feeling a little unsettled about her art and welcomes the daunting challenge of starting over for each book with a new art medium or technique for the sake of illustrating it in the most compelling possible way. When she and I spoke in her Brooklyn apartment on January 15, 2014, Novgorodoff had recently completed *The Undertaking of Lily Chen,* a sprawling tale of intrigue and noirish adventure set in contemporary China. She had visited China (her second time there) to research the project and seemed pleased to be able to report that in one rural village where she and a friend had stayed overnight, she and her companion had been briefly mistaken for ghosts.

●　●

Leonard S. Marcus: What were you like as a child?

Danica Novgorodoff: I was a very quiet kid. I enjoyed being alone a lot and going out for a walk with my dog for hours. At one point my family had an eighty-three-acre farm in Michigan. Without an alarm clock, I would wake myself up at six or seven o'clock, before my parents and my twin brother and sister were up, just to have some time to myself. I'm still pretty shy.

Q: Did you like to draw then?

A: Oh, yes. I didn't draw better than any other kid, but my mom says that from the time I could hold a pencil I would draw for hours. My parents set up a little easel for me in the kitchen, and I was glued to it! I remember one of the first books I made in elementary school, about the adventures of a group of magical fire-wielding alien ponies. I had been doodling horses for years, so my full-page alien horse illustrations were pretty darn good. My parents helped me put it together into a book with a plastic comb binding pilfered from my mom's office. I felt like a true author.

Q: Were horses a big part of your childhood, too?

A: A huge part. Every little girl is obsessed with ponies, but I have been riding since I was about seven years old, and by the time I was in high school, we were living in Kentucky. I would also draw horses all the time. Horses have made their way into most of my books. Even now I keep seeking out situations where I can ride, so I guess I've never given that up.

Q: Are drawing and riding linked for you in any way?

A: I wonder. Maybe in a roundabout way. The way that you communicate with a horse is sort of abstract. It's beyond language, in the same way that art is beyond language. Communicating with a horse—telling the horse what you want and need it to do—is all done through feel and instinct and intuition. Making an image is a lot like that. An awareness of your own body is also very important to riding horses. You have to know exactly what your body is doing—its position and breathing. I find that when I'm riding a horse, it clears my mind of literal thoughts and helps me to think creatively.

Q: How did you find your way into the world of graphic novels?

A: I started college with the idea that I would be an art major "unless something better came up," and I never found anything I liked better. But I didn't start making or reading graphic novels until toward the end of college. I was a painter and photographer when an artist friend introduced me to comics. He not only put comics-style panels in his paintings but also drew a weekly strip for the student newspaper. My paintings were always narrative, and I liked to write short stories. So it all came together for me in comics. The first graphic novel I ever read was Art Spiegelman's *Maus,* probably also in senior year.

After graduation I traveled in South America for half a year. I wanted to do an art project while I was away that could travel with me and that would come together as a book by the end of my journey. I wanted to have something to show for my time away. That is when I made my first comic. It was called *Neck of the Moon,* after the Kichwa name for the volcano I was living near in Ecuador, and it grew to more than a hundred pages. It was probably the most experimental and messiest thing I have ever made! It is not necessarily readable, but it was a great way to start.

Q: Then what happened?

A: After returning from South America, I moved to New York, and I used that strange little book I had done to show people. I began to meet other graphic novelists and was hired as the designer at First Second Books, which was quite new at the time. At that point I began to get pretty involved in the graphic novel world.

Q: What did you learn from the authors/artists whose books you designed?

A: I had actually made a couple of my own books before I started working on other artists' books, so I think my own work informed my editing at the same time that I got ideas from looking closely at other people's books. It's always interesting to see other artists' processes—how they plan, how they think, what kind of sketches they make, how many hours they work in a day, how much they demand of themselves, how many sheets of paper they throw away, how they use technology, their favorite white-out, where they get their inspiration, and so forth. I like to try out a new process when it looks like it's working well for someone else. It's been helpful for me to see other artists who really take their studio time seriously—I even know one artist who punches in on a clock!—and I've always tried to guard my work time as sacred, even though I'm my own boss and I work in a home studio.

Last year I taught a graphic novel class at an art school and had a student who simply didn't think in a linear way. His comic panels were not sequential moments in time but rather squares in the grid on a map, or cars of a train, or sections of a body. That kind of blew my rational mind and inspired me to think more creatively about time and space in graphic novels.

Q: Why did you want to tell the story that became your first published book, *Slow Storm*?

A: *Slow Storm* was inspired by the life stories of some people I knew from Kentucky. I used to work at a horse barn, and a lot of the guys who worked there were Mexican immigrants. I became friends with them. I had another friend who was a firefighter. So the story came out of those friendships and out of the Kentucky landscape, which I missed, having recently moved away from there.

Q: What about the book that came next?

A: *Refresh, Refresh* is based on a film script and short story, both written by Benjamin Percy. I first read the story in 2007 or 2008. The United States had already been involved in the wars in Iraq and Afghanistan for many years, and I started to think about how a lot of kids had grown up with those wars in the background of their entire childhood. Because the wars were, and continue to be, a huge backdrop to all of American life, I thought it was an important story to tell. And I thought that although I had not been a soldier and had never even visited the Middle East, I could still tell this powerful story about the people, and especially the kids, who were dealing

Turf

by Danica Novgorodoff

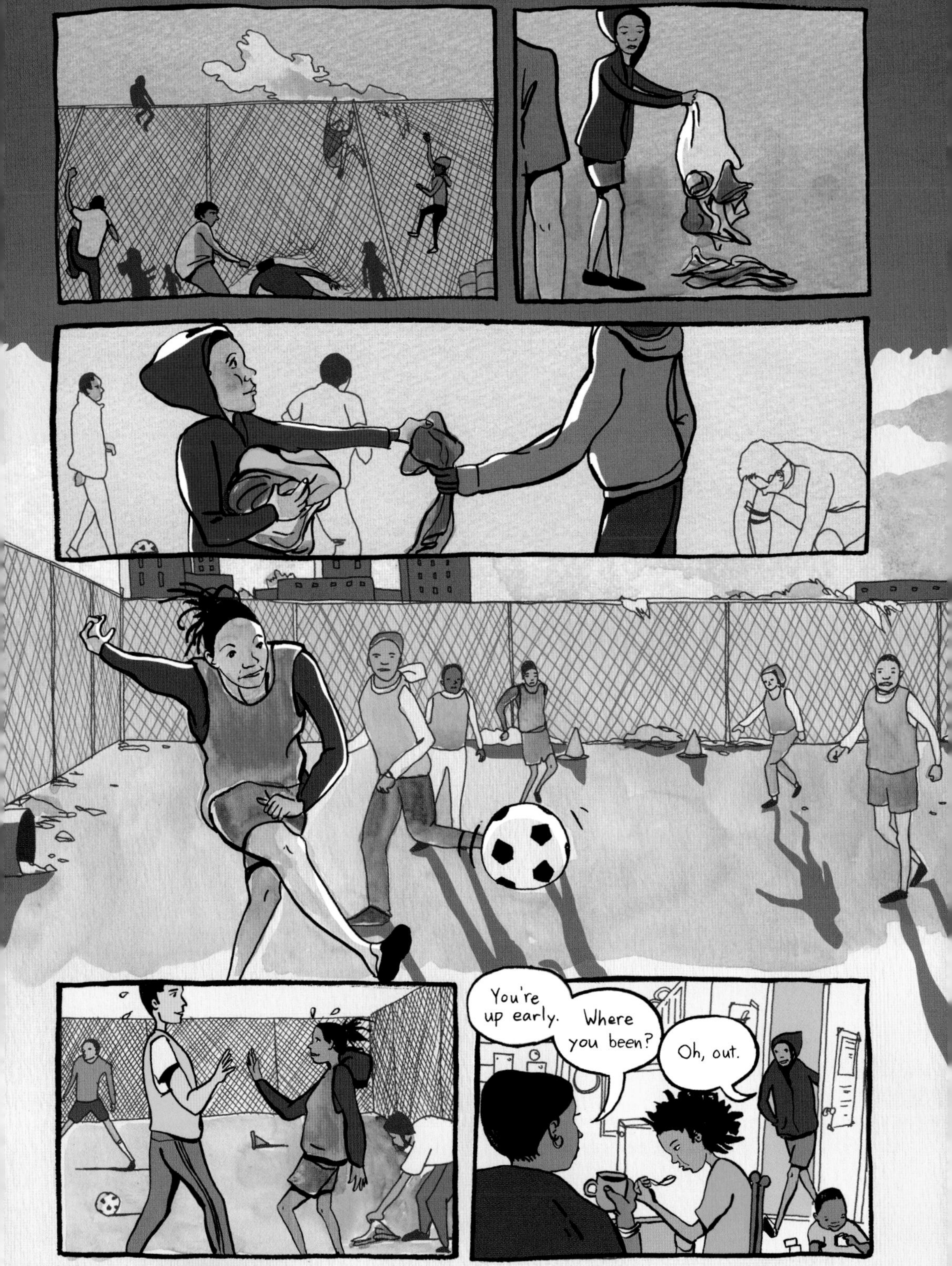
You're up early.
Where you been?
Oh, out.

with the wars as they lived their daily lives in their hometowns. I love that the story starts with the boys playing fighting games and that as the story unfolds and the seasons change, their situation gets more and more dire. One kid's father dies; another kid is having problems just keeping his household running while his mom works two jobs. As time passes, the boys' games turn more violent. It's one way to describe a coming of age, though not a very hopeful one, I guess. I tried to show what it was like for them, without being didactic. I wanted readers to decide for themselves what they thought about it.

Q: Do you do research for your books?

A: It's important to me to get the feeling of a place I'm drawing. For *Slow Storm,* that was easy. Being from Kentucky, I went and photographed a landscape that was already familiar to me. While I was there, I visited a firehouse and photographed the fire trucks from every possible angle, and I went back to the barn where I used to ride horses and used it as a model for various of the book's scenes.

For *Refresh, Refresh,* I went to the small town in Oregon where the story takes place. I had been planning to spend a week there, but on the first day, I found that it took just ten minutes to walk from one end of the town to the other. I thought, "OK, this is it? What am I going to do here for a week?" But it turned out to be important to get to know the place well. In all my books, the landscapes matter as much as the characters.

Q: Are there some things you find especially hard to draw?

A: Cars, and vehicles in general. That's because they have such a specific geometry. If you get it wrong, it really *looks* wrong. Whereas if you draw a tree, if you get the angle of the tree wrong, it still looks like a tree. I also have trouble with interiors and other scenes involving precise perspective. I prefer drawing things that are looser and more organic.

Q: Your third graphic novel takes place in China. Did you set yourself a particular challenge as you began working on it?

A: I wanted the art for *The Undertaking of Lily Chen* to suggest Chinese brush painting. I began my research by studying the ancient scroll paintings and ink drawings and landscape paintings of the Chinese masters. I also took a Chinese brush-painting class for a couple of semesters. Before the course actually began, I had thought, "I'll just take a class or two and will then have all the technique I need for my graphic novel." The teacher started us out on painting bamboo. We did this for *several* weeks. Then she had us paint some flowers. I said to the teacher, "I want to paint mountains. I want to paint landscapes!" At which point she gave me this look and said, "Well, first you have to learn to paint a rock." "OK," I said. "Sure." That is when I found out that I had no idea how to paint a rock, that it was so difficult. I realized that that was why people study brush painting for seventy years. So I gave up on becoming a master of Chinese brush painting, and I figured that I could at least use the techniques I was learning to reference Chinese brush painting in my book. That is what I did do.

Q: You also visited China.

A: I have been to mainland China twice. The first time I was still working full-time at First Second Books and did not yet have plans to make a book set in China. I had two weeks of vacation coming to me, and I had thought, "Where's the farthest place I can possibly go, geographically and culturally, in two weeks' time?"

It's true that I have a Chinese grandmother and that my dad was born there. But China felt very foreign to me when an adventurous

As Danica Novgorodoff honed her comic, she not only specified
more background detail . . .

friend of mine, who was living there at the time, and I decided to
travel together through the southern Chinese countryside, stopping
in a couple of cities along the way.

One day at around dusk, my friend Tanya and I were out walking past a temple in a small town in Hunan Province. I don't know
why, but a woman who saw us thought we were ghosts. It was
such a small town that it was easy for her to figure out in which
family's home we were staying that night. The woman came by to
investigate, explaining that she had seen us earlier. She then tied
a string around each of our wrists, which I guess somehow ensured

but also moved more action to the foreground and turned more of her characters to face us.

that we were not ghosts after all, though I'm not sure how. I carried many images of that trip back with me, in my mind and also in my camera.

Then a month or two later, I read an article in the *Economist* about the Chinese tradition of "ghost marriages," and I thought, "This would make a really interesting story," which I then began to piece together. About two years later, I went back, this time with *The Undertaking of Lily Chen* in mind, and took a lot of photographs that I thought might be of use for the book.

Q: Why is there so much interest in graphic novels now?

A: I guess it is part of the larger evolution of image-based media. Video games are huge now, along with movies—everything that combines text and images.

Q: Do you see a strong connection between film and graphic novels?

A: For me, yes, there's a big connection. When I was writing the script for *The Undertaking of Lily Chen,* I would envision each scene as a scene in a film. Sometimes I would have to stop myself and realize, "This is not going to work in a drawing. I am going to have to write it differently." I wrote a scene, for instance, with an empty gray stone city in which mist was rising through the streets. I thought, "You can't actually make mist rise in a drawing, can you?" I tried it and it didn't work out nearly as well as it had in my mind! It would have looked beautiful in a film.

Q: Many of the full-page illustrations in your books could easily stand alone as pictures on an art gallery wall.

A: I like to make comics one image at a time. I understand that another way to make comics is to have each image work more as a bit of handwriting or as a device for moving the narrative forward, rather than as something to dwell on as an individual piece of art. You have to play with the different possibilities and make sure you have the right balance of artwork that advances the story and artwork that is simply beautiful to look at and linger over.

Q: Tell me about "Turf."

A: The inspiration for my comic "Turf" is a morning pickup soccer game I've been playing for years in Brooklyn. We call ourselves

"Sunrise FC"—"FC" for "Football Club." The crowd is diverse and includes a number of high school kids who come out to play before class or in the summer. We take over an empty Astroturf field at the edge of Prospect Park for an hour several times a week. It's the city version of my own childhood morning routine—get up and "hit the streets"—whether Astroturf or cornfield—before everyone else wakes up, at that amazing sunrise hour.

Q: What do you like best about making graphic novels?

A: I love the potential for experimentation, all the different ways you can combine words and images. I like the different types of pacing you can have: the expanses of space and time, and the moments of silence and moments of great action that you can fit into a single page. It's a very versatile form. The text and images can be paired to tell the same story in two completely different ways, or they can tell two different stories simultaneously. When I made *Slow Storm,* I had never used watercolor before. I chose watercolor because I thought it would work well with that particular story, which, being about a storm, is moody and wet and lush. The Kentucky landscape is very green and loose, so I thought it would be best rendered in water-color. But because I had never used watercolor, I had to experiment and to throw away a lot of pages before I got ones that worked for my book.

I love books because of the possibility for anyone to see them and read them. If you have a gallery show, it goes up for a month and the couple of hundred people who happen to walk into the gallery will see it. Whereas a book lives on indefinitely as a reproducible object, and you never know who is going to read it.

MATT PHELAN

(Born 1970, Drexel Hill, Pennsylvania)

Some artists and writers know exactly who they are and where they are headed from the moment they can hold a paintbrush or clasp a pencil. Lucky them! Not Matt Phelan. Before he was an illustrator, Phelan spent several years as a bookseller. Before he was a bookseller, he tried his luck at acting. No experience, they say, is ever lost on a curious, broad-minded person, however, and selling picture books year after year opened Phelan's eyes to the exciting work being done by illustrators like Lane Smith in *The Stinky Cheese Man* and William Joyce in *A Day with Wilbur Robinson.* Seeing those books was enough to convince Phelan that he wanted to be part of that world. There was just one problem. Phelan did not know how to draw! He spent the next five years teaching himself to draw like an illustrator. It was a big challenge that called for a great deal of patience, hard work, and discipline. As Phelan struggled to learn how to draw a character with feeling, his acting experience came in handy, too.

Then Phelan got lucky. Just as publishers were discovering him as an illustrator, they were also discovering the graphic novel as an exciting new type of book. Suddenly the search was on for artists who understood the new storytelling form. Phelan, it turned out, was a step ahead of them and was already well into the making of *The Storm in the Barn*. Begun as a just-for-fun after-hours experiment, *The Storm in the Barn* made perfect sense to librarians, booksellers, and critics by the time it was published in 2009. It won the next year's Scott O'Dell Award for historical fiction—a first for a graphic novel—that not only put Phelan on the map but also helped many to see for the first time that comics were as well suited to nonfiction as they were to fantasy.

Phelan was home in the nifty studio shed he built in his suburban Philadelphia backyard when we recorded this conversation by phone on November 7, 2013.

. . . .

Leonard S. Marcus: What were you like growing up?

Matt Phelan: For some reason, I was always interested in the behind-the-scenes story of things. I realized at an early age that books were made by people and that people did all kinds of other creative work for a living as well. When *Star Wars* came out, I was interested in all the special effects, and I knew that model builders were responsible for many of them. I loved the Muppets and would wonder, "How are Muppets made?" I grew up liking comics and enjoying drawing, but with no burning desire to do comics later. In college I studied theater and film, not art.

Q: What were the first comics you read?

A: I grew up in the 1970s, which was a great time for reprints of comics from earlier decades. My dad would buy me the ones he had read, like Alex Raymond's *Flash Gordon* and Hal Foster's *Prince Valiant*. I also read *Peanuts*. For a time I wanted to be Charles Schulz! Then I "dropped out" for a while. In my twenties, I got back in as a fan of Jeff Smith's *Bone*, which I thought was so well drawn and so funny.

Q: How far did you go as an actor?

A: As with everything else, I liked the behind-the-scenes process of acting more than I liked the applause. I enjoyed figuring out who my character was and how to block out the action onstage. After college I auditioned for a couple of movies and made the short list for one called *Swing Kids* but didn't get the part. Another time I lined up to audition for Francis Ford Coppola for a film he was planning based on Jack Kerouac's *On the Road.* We all had to wait outdoors for hours on a cold miserable day. After maybe four hours, a casting director pointed to a few people, and I was not one of them. I noticed just then that Francis Ford Coppola was nearby, seated in a chair, so I decided to say hi. After all, I had nothing to lose! He was friendly and nice, but when I told him I had not been picked, he said, "Oh well." And that is when I realized that acting was not for me.

Q: Then what did you do?

A: During my twenties, I worked at bookstores and as a copywriter at a university, but I wouldn't let go of the idea that I wanted to do something more creative. In my early thirties, I was still thinking about what that something might be.

From my time at bookstores, I knew about all the great picture books by Lane Smith, William Joyce, and others that were being published. I wanted to make picture books too, but I knew that my drawing skills were not good enough. So I spent about five years studying drawing on my own and putting together a portfolio. I especially liked some of the old drawing books I found. They were tough as nails and would offer suggestions like: "I must advise you to buy your own skeleton." Then I joined a group for writers and illustrators and went to one of their events, where I met an art director who turned out to be interested in working with me.

Q: Five years is a long time. How did you handle the uncertainty of not knowing whether your efforts would pay off?

A: I tried to ignore the uncertainty of what exactly I was going to do. I held an unshakable belief that I'd somehow make a living doing *something* creative. I wanted to be a children's book illustrator above all else, but I was realistic about the challenges involved. As I studied art books during my lunch hour and drew daily, I realized that the pursuit itself was a good thing. I was learning about something I loved. I was incrementally getting better. Even if I never managed to break into publishing, I'd still have that experience of learning to draw, and that in itself was improving my quality of life. That's an important theme in *Bluffton,* too. The conversation Henry has with Sally about the various "ordinary" folks they know who paint or play music for the sheer enjoyment of it is crucial to the story. You don't have to be a professional to benefit from pursuing creative work.

Q: Did you see a connection between your acting experience and your new career as an illustrator?

A: Absolutely. One of the great Disney animators kept a sign on his desk that read "What is the character thinking?" That became my approach to drawing during the years when I was struggling to learn to draw. It meant that I could use my acting experience as an artist.

Q: What led you into the world of graphic novels?

A: At first I saw myself as a picture book artist. Then I had the idea for *The Storm in the Barn.* I tried writing the story as a prose novel that would have one illustration per chapter. I wrote six pages, but they just sat there and felt very static to me. That is when I realized that I could say exactly the same thing, only more interestingly, in a sequence of three drawings. So I decided to tell the story in comics format. When I first had this idea, publishers, it seemed, weren't that interested in graphic novels for kids. But I was lucky because by the time I had nearly finished the book, things had changed and there was a whole lot of interest.

By then I had read the British picture book artist Raymond Briggs's *Ethel and Ernest*, which is a graphic novel about his parents' life together. It knocked me over because it was drawn in Briggs's familiar picture book style, so it didn't look like a typical comic except for the format, and because it was a small, quiet book that nonetheless packed a surprisingly big punch emotionally. I thought, "Wow, he pulled off something amazing." I thought, "This is what a graphic novel can do." And it showed me that I didn't have to draw like a comics artist to draw a graphic novel.

Q: What was it about the story of the Dust Bowl that attracted you?

A: When I was a kid, my dad had coffee-table books of photographs from the Great Depression era. I would stare at the black-and-white pictures, which seemed so stark and beautiful and strange. When I came to the photographs of the Dust Bowl, I remember thinking, "This looks like a different planet. Here's a farm, but there are no crops, no anything. Here's a 200-foot-high black cloud of dust bearing down on a small truck that is trying to keep just ahead of it." There was so much inherent drama in all that, and the portraits are so powerful, with the people of the Dust Bowl usually staring straight into the camera. You can't look away from them. As a kid, all this fascinated me and it stuck with me.

I'd also been interested in the idea of an American fairy tale. What kind of story would that be? We have our traditional Jack tales and we have the Oz books. And I thought if ever there was a land that seemed like it was under a curse, it was the Dust Bowl during the Great Depression. So the story for me had a sort of fairy-tale feel.

CITY LIFE

by Matt Phelan

In the city

there are millions of people,

thousands of things to do.

But on one day each year,

there is only one neighborhood,

one block,

one party.

Q: How big a role did the photographs play when it came time to illustrate your book?

A: I didn't base the drawings directly on those old photographs, but I looked at them so much that I hoped they would seep into my drawings. I approached the illustrations more as an actor would, asking myself, "What is the character thinking? How does the character feel?" I realized, for instance, that Jack's father is not a bad guy, even though he is really hard on his son. His whole world is falling apart, and he doesn't know what to do about it. So I tried to draw him as a man who feels completely lost.

Q: Your drawings don't look all that much like photographs.

A: I like my drawings to be a little sketchy. I wouldn't want any panel to be so fully rendered that someone would stop reading and say, "Oh, look at this. Let's stare at this picture for a while." I don't want you to stop. I want the reader to keep going because the scene is still going.

Q: It's interesting that the young heroes of two of your books — Jack in *The Storm in the Barn* and Buster Keaton in *Bluffton* — don't have real childhoods in the ordinary sense.

A: Jack is sort of stuck in time. He can't be a carefree child because of the Depression, and he doesn't have a chance to prove himself because the family farm has been knocked out of commission by the Dust Bowl drought. In some ways, Buster is the opposite of Jack. He's already a star and he's mostly locked into that role. But Buster himself always said that he loved his childhood, even though he didn't get to hang out with other kids his own age in the usual way. The summer months that he spent in Bluffton were the exception, when he came closest to being a regular kid, so telling that story was a way to show his human side: Buster when he was not completely caught up in being a performer.

Q: Do you see your child self in any of the child characters you've created?

A: Yes. In *Bluffton* Henry is me. He was a very easy character for me to write. For a long time I tried to think of the story of *Bluffton* from Buster's point of view, but it didn't work. Then I realized it had to be told from the point of view of an ordinary kid who sees these vaude-villians come to town every summer. Once I figured that out, every-thing else quickly fell into place. I thought to myself, "How would I have felt when I was twelve if I had met this kid who could stand still, then jump in the air and flip backward, and who wouldn't teach me how to do it?"

Q: Do you have a work routine?

A: I work from eight or nine until about three. I have a backyard stu-dio, and once I cross the yard from the house and go inside, I'm at work. I always have in mind what I want to do in a given day. Because graphic novels tend to be so large, it's important to have a daily schedule or plan.

I write a script before I do any drawing for my books. Having the story locked down allows me to draw scenes out of sequence if I want to, for instance, to put off drawing a really complicated scene until I feel ready to do it, or to schedule some of the lightest scenes at the end, when I might be feeling burned out.

Q: How many stages are there?

A: First there may be a lot of preliminary reading and research. Before I had the idea for *Around the World,* I had been collecting books for a

These two early thumbnail studies both feature a glimpse of a tall building that Matt Phelan later discarded, as he realized his comic was going to be about the intimate sights and pleasures of neighborhood life within a big city.

good ten years about people who made solo around-the-world journeys. I kept reading these books, and finally I realized that many of the journeys they described had taken place within the same fifteen-year period, around the turn of the last century. This in itself struck me as fascinating, and it gave me the idea to retell three of the stories in a book.

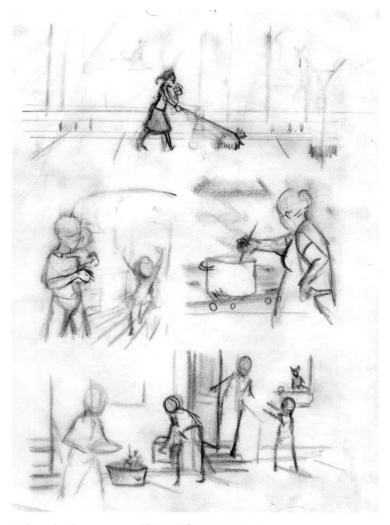

In these sketches, page one of "City Life" starts to take shape.

Once I have my story, I write a complete script. Then I do the first drawings—detailed thumbnail sketches of the entire book. That's my favorite stage because that is when all the important decisions are made: decisions about not only the images themselves but also the size of the panels and the flow of the story. The drawings are very simple at that stage, so there's not a lot of pressure. But you can get all the information you need into a stick figure! Then my editor and I go over everything, and I start doing the final art. By then all the serious thinking and planning has been done.

Q: Tell me about the comic you created for this book, "City Life."

A: I lived in a row house in South Philadelphia for nine years, during which time I illustrated my first twenty-one books, including my three graphic novels. My two children were born in the city as well. I really enjoyed the smaller moments of city life, like strolling to neighborhood parks with my kids and bumping into friends with their kids. We lived on a block with some wonderful neighbors, and it was a really close-knit community. Each year my street had a fantastic block party that brought everyone out, and on that day the whole city was that small block for me.

Q: What do you enjoy most about making graphic novels?

A: Each book has its own challenges. I always try to let the story determine how I am going to draw the story. In *Around the World,* I used a different drawing style for each of the three stories I tell. For the last one, which is about Joshua Slocum, I drew it in pen and ink because I thought of Slocum as a kind of exposed nerve: a man who because he is haunted by the death of his wife can no longer live on land. I realized that with pen and ink, I could make drawings that had that same nervous energy. I used a beautiful old pen that I bought at a sidewalk sale in Philadelphia. I beat the hell out of it because I wanted everything in the drawings to be scratchy-looking. If you push a pen like that too hard, you might splatter the ink. Usually that's not a good thing, but in this book I wanted that to happen because the splatter became the spray of the water or the energy of Slocum himself, who haunted and fascinated me. Slocum wasn't a very talkative man, any more than Jack's father was in *The Storm* *in the Barn.* The graphic novel is a good art form for telling stories about someone like that because you can zero in on the character's facial expressions even if little is being said in words.

For *Bluffton* I needed the illustrations to have the special quality of summer light, and nothing is better for showing that than watercolor. Watercolor, though, can be so many different things. I had to study the medium in order to be able to use it well. It can be very precise, as in David Wiesner's picture books. Or it can be this loose and crazy thing. It can be very loose or it can be semi-loose. Part of what it has taken me nine years to realize is that watercolor only starts working well if you are willing to let it do what it's going to do, and let go a little bit. The accidents are more than half of what watercolor is all about. That can be scary. You have to be prepared to lay it down and if necessary to try again. When I'm drawing with watercolor, I always think, "Well, here goes. I hope this works!"

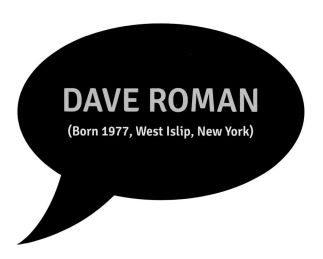

DAVE ROMAN

(Born 1977, West Islip, New York)

Dave Roman counts himself lucky not to have had to fight the old battles familiar to previous generations of comics fans and creators. Far from pressuring him to trade in his favorite childhood reading for "real" books, Roman's parents and teachers were great about feeding his interest. When he started to write and draw comics himself, they cheered him on. Roman met graphic novelist Raina Telgemeier at art school and proposed to her midflight on an airplane by presenting her with a handmade comic in which he popped the question on the next-to-last page. He had left the last page blank for her to write in her response. Telgemeier—the author of *Smile, Drama,* and *Sisters*— scribbled "Yes!" Although no longer married, Roman and Telgemeier came of age professionally together and in 2011 were even profiled by *The New York Times* as a rising comics-world power couple. Ten years earlier, media attention at that level would have been unimaginable for any graphic novelist whose name was not Art Spiegelman.

After college Roman answered *Scooby-Doo* fan mail as a DC Comics intern before joining the editorial staff at *Nickelodeon Magazine.* It was an exciting job that for ten years put him in contact with a worldwide array of comics artists and writers. Getting to know their work helped Roman sift through the many options open to him as he searched for his own creative voice and style.

These days Roman puts the stamp of his pert, oddball sense of humor on everything he does, whether he is working solo or collaboratively. The chance to team up with an artist friend seems for him to be the most enjoyable aspect of being a citizen in good standing of the world comics community. As Roman told me when we recorded this conversation in the living room of his Brooklyn apartment on December 13, 2013, he also gets great satisfaction from meeting young fans—and, if making comics is what they really dream of doing, urging them to have the courage to try.

• •

Leonard S. Marcus: How did you discover comics?

Dave Roman: I began as a fan of newspaper comic strips—*Peanuts, Garfield, Dennis the Menace*—whatever was in our local newspaper. Then one day I bought a *Garfield* collection at a school book fair. The experience of seeing the daily strips brought together in that way and of following a story in sequence from page to page made me fall in love with comics. After that I wanted to read as many comic strips as possible. I sought out other newspapers, hoping to find strips that were not published in ours. I began to copy the strips too.

Q: Then what happened?

A: When I was in fifth or sixth grade, my dad took me to a comics shop. The owner introduced me to comics that he thought would appeal to me as a fan of the strips: *Scrooge McDuck* by Carl Barks and *Groo the Wanderer*, a fantasy series by Sergio Aragonés, who is best known for doing *Mad* magazine. By then I was also drawing my own comics.

I figured out quickly that a comic book wouldn't be too hard to make at home: all it took was paper and staples. I would ask my parents to photocopy the comic books I drew at their office. At first I sold them to family members. Then in junior high I sold them at the school store. I was determined to become a comic book mogul! By high school my friends and I were going to comics conventions and taking a table at which we showed off our wares. Of course, we made no money whatsoever. We just needed to get our comics out there and into people's hands.

Q: What were your comics like in those days?

A: I had a character named Rad Brad. He was rad!—and looked something like the characters in *Calvin and Hobbes.* I also had a cast of farm characters called *The Funny Farm.* They looked like *Garfield* characters. I would take a style and create new characters in it. In junior high I was doing a book called *Samurai Jack,* about a kid samurai warrior. That was inspired by Sergio Aragonés.

Q: Apparently, your father was fine with your interest in comics.

A: I was pretty fortunate in that regard. My immediate family and friends were supportive and my teachers even more so. In junior high the teachers encouraged me to draw a comic strip for the school paper.

Q: Did you have other artists in your family?

A: One of my uncles was known as "the artist of the family." People would say that I was following in his footsteps. He wasn't a professional artist, but he had painted when he was younger and he drew very well.

Another relative gave me a book called *How to Draw Comics the Marvel Way*. This was *the* how-to book for superhero comics artists. It had sections on "dynamic anatomy," "action poses," "how to show people being thrown through a window"—all that kind of exciting stuff. I liked to read superhero comics, but I found that as an artist I was better at drawing humor comics and things with simpler character designs. I had a little bit of an identity crisis. For a long time, I felt I was doing a kind of dance between the two styles as I tried to figure myself out as an artist.

Q: Did Art Spiegelman's *Maus* change the way you and your friends thought about comics?

A: The two books that are often mentioned as game-changers are *Maus* and *The Dark Knight Returns* by Frank Miller, *Maus* even more so because it was not a superhero book and because it was a comic about historical events. In my senior year of high school, I took a history test for which we had to choose from a selection of readings. *Maus*, a graphic novel, was one of the choices. That in itself was amazing to me. As a reader, I was blown away by *Maus*. But it didn't seem like the kind of thing I would ever do. I kept gravitating toward whimsy and fantasy.

Q: What did you study at art school? What future did you imagine for yourself?

A: In my freshman year at the School of Visual Arts, everyone took foundation classes in painting, sculpture, and photography. My painting teacher was honest with me. He told me that my painting, which I was trying to do realistically, was weak at best, but that the drawings he found in my notebooks and sketchbooks—the things that I was doodling in the margins—had real life and spirit to them. His comment opened a door for me. It made me realize that I had to channel what I was doing when I was loose and not trying so hard. After that I switched my major from classical illustration to cartooning.

But this was in the mid-nineties, when the comics industry was in an economic downturn. The cartooning teachers at SVA were all saying not to count on the comics industry for a job. In the past the idea had been to get a job after graduation at Marvel or DC or Archie Comics, or to try to launch a newspaper comic strip of your own. The graphic novel explosion hadn't happened yet, so I didn't realize I could create long-form comics and get paid for it.

As it happened, immediately after college I was hired by Nickelodeon to be the assistant to their three comics editors. I stayed for ten years, and as time went on, I did more and more editing myself. I worked with artists from around the world. It was really exciting. By the time I left, I had also gained more confidence in my own drawing ability. I felt ready to be on my own.

Q: What did you do next?

A: My comics friends and I had all gotten used to the idea that we were not going to make any money from comics, that creating them was basically an exciting kind of hobby. Cartoonists were just starting to put their work on the Internet, which was a new way to self-publish your work that was completely free. The Internet became a new underground comix scene. The variety of what was out there was amazing. I decided to try it too. I met a great many people that way, including editors who wanted to publish me. The Internet turned out to be a great way to become known.

Q: How did the current explosion of interest in graphic novels get started?

A: Part of it had to do with the impact of the Internet, which allowed

THE PROXIMITY EFFECT
by Dave Roman

When I tell someone that I'm from New York, they probably imagine:

JUST LIKE IN THE MOVIES!

But where I grew up, it was much more:

LIKE ON A TV SITCOM!

The distance between Long Island and Manhattan really depends on your *PERSPECTIVE.*

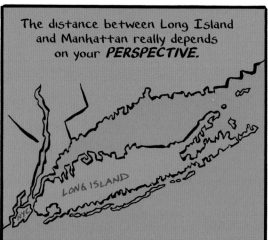

LONG ISLAND

NYC

For some, the city is a faraway, scary place.

Can I go on the class trip to see "Cats" on Broadway?

Only if you bring pepper spray and promise not to get mugged.

GO BAG

My parents were raised in Brooklyn, and always talked about *ESCAPING* the streets for a better life in the suburbs.

I was in a rough Puerto Rican gang! Just like "West Side Story"!

And it's hard to argue with the benefits of growing up with your own backyard.

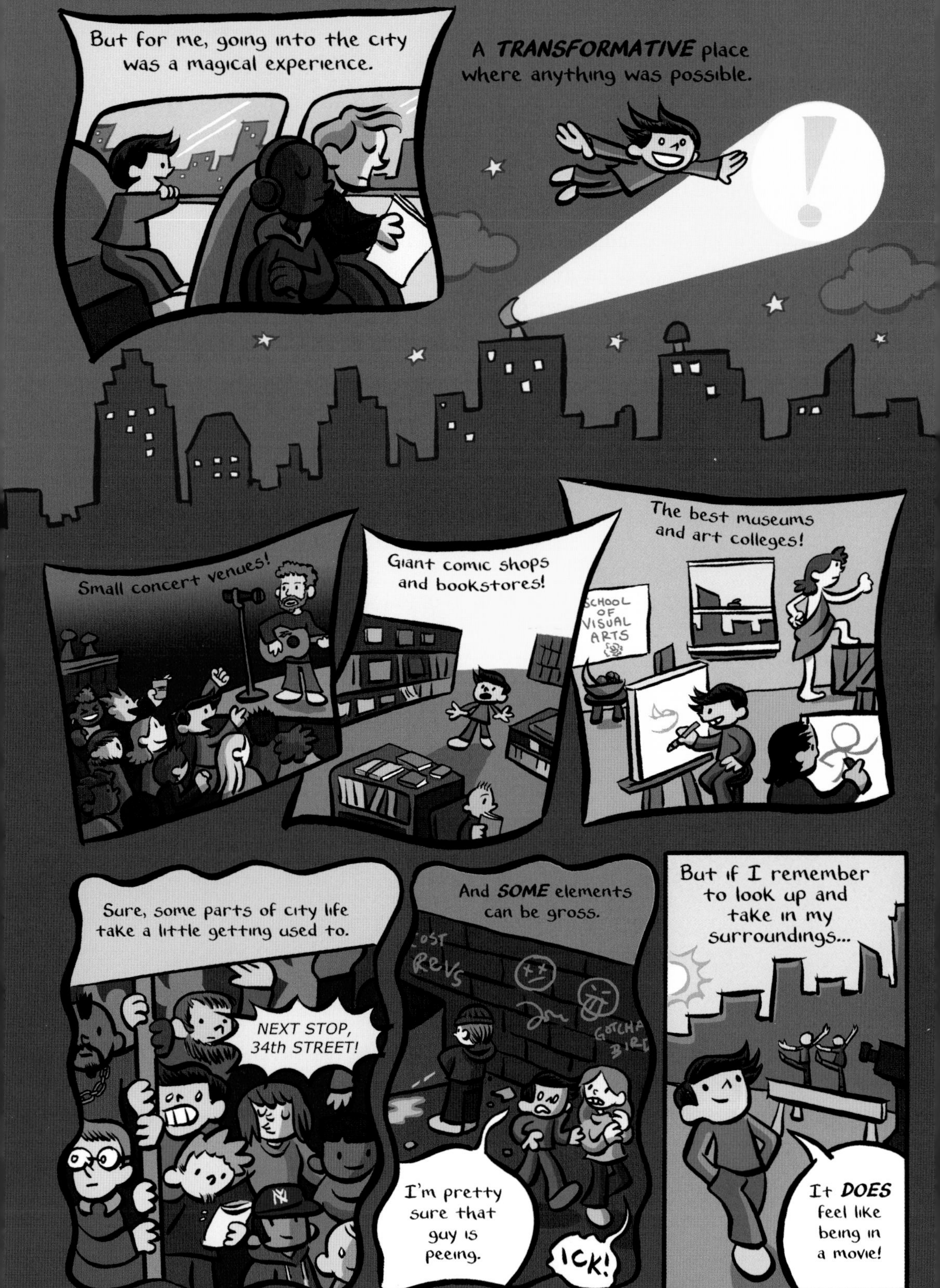
But for me, going into the city was a magical experience.
A *TRANSFORMATIVE* place where anything was possible.
Small concert venues!
Giant comic shops and bookstores!
The best museums and art colleges!
SCHOOL OF VISUAL ARTS
Sure, some parts of city life take a little getting used to.
NEXT STOP, 34th STREET!
And *SOME* elements can be gross.
REVS
GOTCHA BIRD
I'm pretty sure that guy is peeing.
ICK!
But if I remember to look up and take in my surroundings...
It *DOES* feel like being in a movie!

people from all over the world to connect through their comics. Historically, the comics industry had been male dominated and largely obsessed with superheroes. It seemed like it was either that or nothing. Most of the books being published were targeted to a male audience. But when Japanese comics, some of which were aimed at girls, started being imported to the U.S., people saw that comics could speak to many different audiences. That helped to open things up, and more women started making comics. So many new voices have come into comics. Then the children's book publishers suddenly became interested in comics too. So there were many factors that all came together. For a long time, people associated comics just with superheroes. It seems like it was either that or nothing. But now comics are no longer just a genre, but a format within which you can tell any kind of story.

Q: What kinds of stories do you like to tell?

A: I grew up with the Muppets and *Sesame Street.* They provided me with the ladder to Mel Brooks and movies like *Airplane!* As a kid, I loved seeing familiar things skewered. I loved satire.

The Teen Boat and Astronaut Academy books are me taking things I love, or genres that I love, and putting a fun spin on them. Astronaut Academy was published first, but both series were created at about the same time. Both started as mini-comics and web comics. The Teen Boat stories were originally done as black-and-white books that we photocopied in hundreds of copies. They found their way into stores and people's hands.

Q: You collaborated on Teen Boat with your friend, comics and video game writer-artist John Green. What was that like?

A: John and I met when I was in high school. We are best friends and have known each other for years and years. We have a sort of shorthand way of communicating when we're working together. John is a little more structured and classical than I am. He'll come up with perfectly formed one-liners and puns, whereas I will think of some really bizarre visual or weird disconnect that to me is very funny. I will say, "Let's have a boy who can transform into a boat," and John will know exactly what type of yacht the boat should be. I sometimes feel like I'm pitching the ball for John to hit out of the park. It takes the humor to another level when you appear to be taking it all so seriously, down to the last detail.

John and I are both primarily kids of the eighties, when transformation fantasies were a huge part of children's entertainment. There were GoBots toys and Transformers and the TV cartoon show about the robot Voltron. There were even teddy bears called Popples that transformed into brightly colored balls. Teen Boat put a spin on all those things, while it was also a good way to talk about adolescence, when you're growing up and your voice is changing and you are having pimples all at the same time. We liked contrasting the cool and not-so-cool aspects of growing up. It's cool to be able to transform into a vehicle. But it's not a really sexy vehicle. It's a fairly small boat.

Q: The title is a pun on "dreamboat."

A: Boats lend themselves to all sorts of nautical humor, not to mention puns like "pier pressure." As a matter of fact, Teen Boat might have just been a joke between friends. A year passed between the long bus ride to a comics convention during which John and I came up with the idea for Teen Boat and the time when we finally said, "You know what? We should actually do that. Let's make it into a little book." We started by making an eight-page photocopied mini-comic. That could have been it too. But the reception was so positive that we thought, "We have to keep going."

Q: You are married to comics artist Raina Telgemeier. Do you and Raina collaborate? Edit each other's work?

A: We help each other when we're stuck. But our books are so different that for the most part we keep things separate. I gravitate toward whimsy, whereas she is so grounded, always pulling from her own life. Because of that, we provide a great checks-and-balances system for each other. I get to be a really big fan of her work and to be the first reader of anything she does, and she is my first reader.

Q: In *Astronaut Academy: Re-Entry*, one of your characters discovers the dictionary and daydreams about spending the rest of his life immersed in a universe of words. Was that a moment taken from your own childhood?

A: A little bit. One of the things that that series is all about is the joy of playing with language. I loved *Monty Python* as a kid. As a teenager, I was already paying close attention to the way that certain comedians would turn a phrase or play with the English language. For Astronaut Academy, I had the idea of writing a comic in which the sentence structure was intentionally off-kilter, almost like a bad translation, and of generating new jokes from the misuse of certain words or expressions.

Q: Do you carry a sketchbook around with you?

A: Yes. I find that a lot of my ideas come from doodling characters over and over. After a while they take on a distinctive shape and personality, and I can start to think about them as people. Once that happens, stories form based on the relationship between the people. Most of my books have started that way.

Dave Roman likes to keep some of the casual feel of sketches like these in his finished art. The text for "The Proximity Effect" is set in a typeface specially designed for him by collaborator John Green. Called "Yaytime," the font is based on the artist's handwriting, as seen here.

Q: Do you revise your work much?

A: Not so much when I'm drawing, because for me the first drawings are usually the ones with the most energy. I want my finishes to feel like sketches, and I find the more I refine a drawing, the more is lost.

Q: Do you have a work routine?

A: I wish I did!

Q: Is there anything that you cannot draw?

A: Lots of things! Animals, cars, architecture, perspective. All the basics! Drawing is a little bit of a struggle for me, and I think it will always feel that way to me. Most people don't realize this, but anytime you write a story, you are potentially introducing thousands of subjects that you have never drawn before.

Q: Tell me about the comic you did for this book, "The Proximity Effect."

A: It's about my relationship to New York City as someone who grew up just outside of the city, on Long Island. New York was always a presence, even though we couldn't see the city from our window. I always knew it was out there and that we were in the shadow of it. I always felt that *that's* where movies take place. That's where the action is. Where I grew up felt more like what you'd see on TV sitcoms like *Leave It to Beaver.* What I found strange, and decided to focus on, was that my parents, who had grown up in Brooklyn, had wanted to move out from the city and that I was drawn toward the city—in the opposite direction. So I tried to show the city as a magical place and a place of bright colors and stars. That's why I have myself flying through the city.

Q: Do you think that comics and film have a lot in common as art forms?

A: People have made that connection, because they're both visual mediums and because a comic looks like a storyboard for a film, even though the two are created for very different purposes. But comics are also related to the traditional prose narrative. They require you to use your imagination to a degree that I think is closer to what it takes to read a novel than to what happens when you watch a film. With comics, even though you are given lots of pictures, you still have to connect what happens in between the frames for yourself. If an author chooses to show a person in a house, and then if in the next scene that person is shown outside the house, your imagination is what connects those moments. In film the frames flow continuously and you see every moment and every detail. You're a more passive viewer. Comics fall somewhere between film and prose narrative.

Q: What is next for comics?

A: A lot of comics people are used to being underdogs and having to struggle. We're used to fighting the system, to justifying our existence! But now librarians tell us stories about how one of our books inspired someone or helped a struggling reader. It's not something we're used to! We're also meeting so many kids who want to make comics, including kids who have been inspired by us. We are really excited about the next generation. What are they going to produce?

This summer I tried to write a traditional novel. As a cartoonist, you tell yourself, "Those guys have it easy. They don't have to draw anything!" But I found out that writing a novel is equally hard, in a different way. I would be writing a scene and struggling to find just the right turn of phrase. That is when I would catch myself thinking, "Can't I just draw this?"

MARK SIEGEL

(Born 1967, Ann Arbor, Michigan)

SIENA CHERSON SIEGEL

(Born 1967, San Juan, Puerto Rico)

By the time Mark Siegel and Siena Cherson met as undergraduates at Brown University, they both knew something about what it is like to chase a big dream. Mark arrived at Brown raring to perfect the skills he had been developing from childhood as an artist and writer—the career he always envisioned for himself. Siena had trained from age six to be a ballerina and had been edging ever closer to that near-impossible goal when at eighteen she suffered an ankle injury that abruptly ended her chances. College for her was about reimagining her life minus the dream that had meant so much to her for as long as she could remember. She met Mark while having a go at acting, in a play written and directed by him.

Although Mark was able to keep to his original plan, it was not smooth sailing for him for a time. About ten years passed after Mark graduated from college before anyone wanted to publish him. (It was not long after *that*, however, that he also became a publisher, founding First Second Books—one of the first imprints to specialize in graphic novels.) In time, Siena decided that teaching young people to dance might be a very good use of her talent. *To Dance* grew out of that same realization. I spoke with Mark and Siena Siegel by phone for this interview on February 16, 2014.

• •

Leonard S. Marcus: What were you like as children?

Mark Siegel: I was a little bit absent, a daydreamer, spending half my life in other worlds.

Siena Cherson Siegel: I was very active and I would say a little bit on the serious side. In terms of dance, I was driven and disciplined. Dance was such a love of mine, though, that much of the time I didn't notice how hard I was working.

Q: Mark, how did you find your way into the world of comics?

M: I was in it as far back as I can remember. I grew up in France and so was exposed first to the European tradition, rather than to American superhero comics or Japanese manga. We were living just outside Paris, and I would read anything and everything I could get my hands on.

At that time there were French magazines for kids that serialized the great French comics artists from the sixties, seventies, and eighties. One magazine, called *Pilote,* was edited by René Goscinny, who also co-created and wrote *Astérix* for the magazine. In all, he produced dozens of series, having been inspired, during a visit to New York, by the gang who launched *Mad. Astérix* got started in the most unlikely way. With just one day left before the first issue of *Pilote* was due to go to the printer, Goscinny realized he had five more pages to fill. So he found an artist who was free named Albert Uderzo and told him they were going to do a comic about a little Gaul warrior. That was the birth of *Astérix,* one of the all-time best-selling comics. Goscinny became a huge role model for me.

Comics were something I always returned to. When I was in third or fourth grade in France, I was already photocopying and selling my comics at school. The first one was about a swarm of mosquitoes. Another was about an invisible man. When I was about nine, I was apprenticed to a painter who had done comics during World War I and worked with Salvador Dalí. [He was] an amazing guy who was in his late eighties when I met him, I think, through a friend of my mother. He took a liking to me. I would draw comics and paint in his studio.

Q: Siena, you were equally passionate about ballet.

S: Yes, and when I realized I wasn't going to be a ballet dancer, I didn't have a backup plan. I did a lot of theater at Brown—which is where Mark and I met—but found I didn't enjoy it. It took several years before I found my work on the education side of dance and thought to write about my own experience.

Q: Mark, when did you start publishing your work?

M: When I came to the States, it was for college. At Brown I studied fine arts and creative writing. After college I had various jobs as a designer while working on my own book and comics projects. I would send them out to publishers and have them rejected—on both sides of the Atlantic! That went on for about ten years. But I was dogged! In 2000 we moved to New York from Boston, and suddenly doors opened for both of us. I illustrated my first picture book, *Seadogs,* in a European comics style, and it got a lot of attention just as publishers were recognizing the exploding popularity in the U.S. of Japanese manga. Publishers at this time were looking for a way to become involved with comics. That in turn led to my starting First Second Books, the comics imprint I continue to edit today at Macmillan.

CITY ENTITY

BY MARK SIEGEL AND SIENA CHERSON SIEGEL

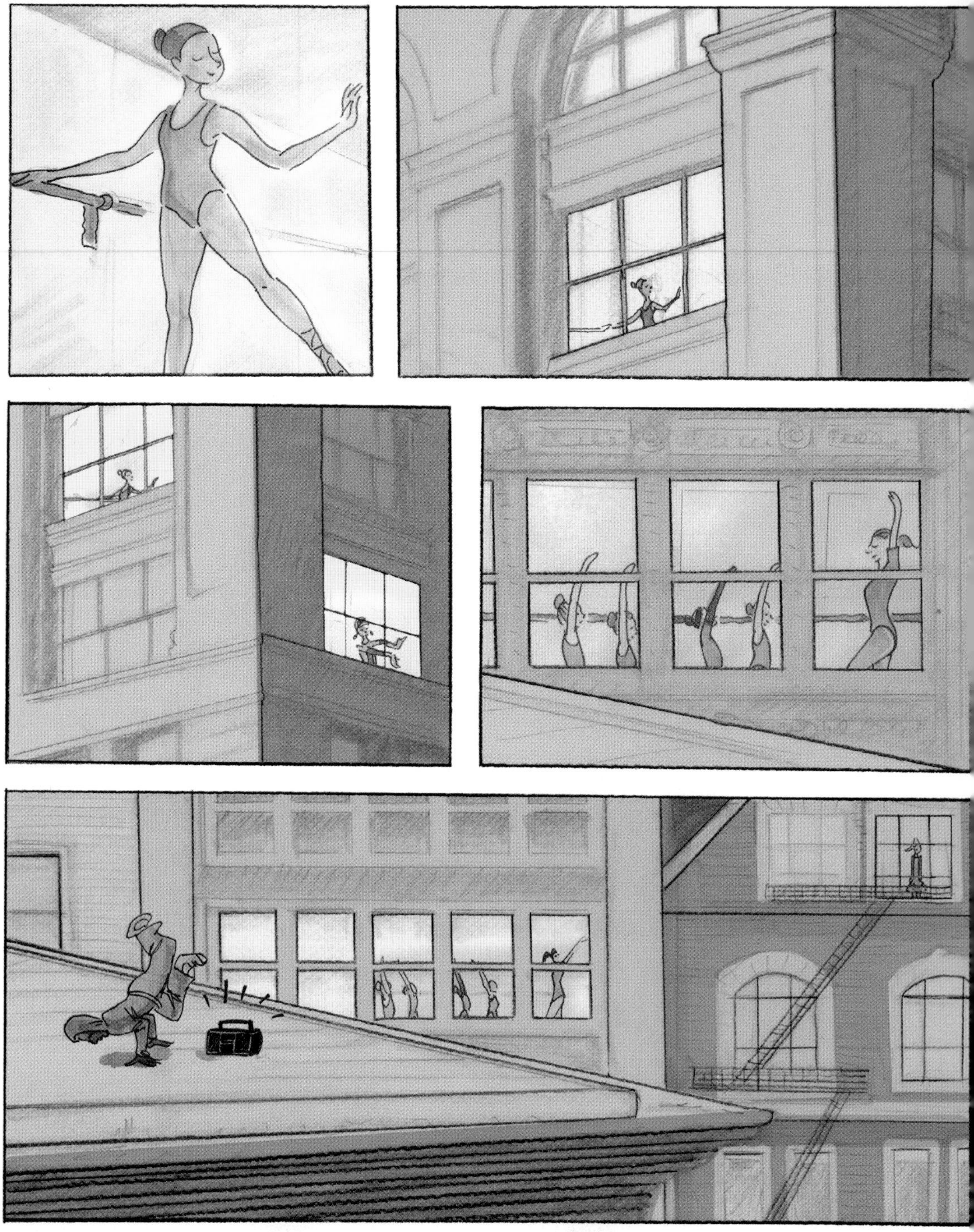

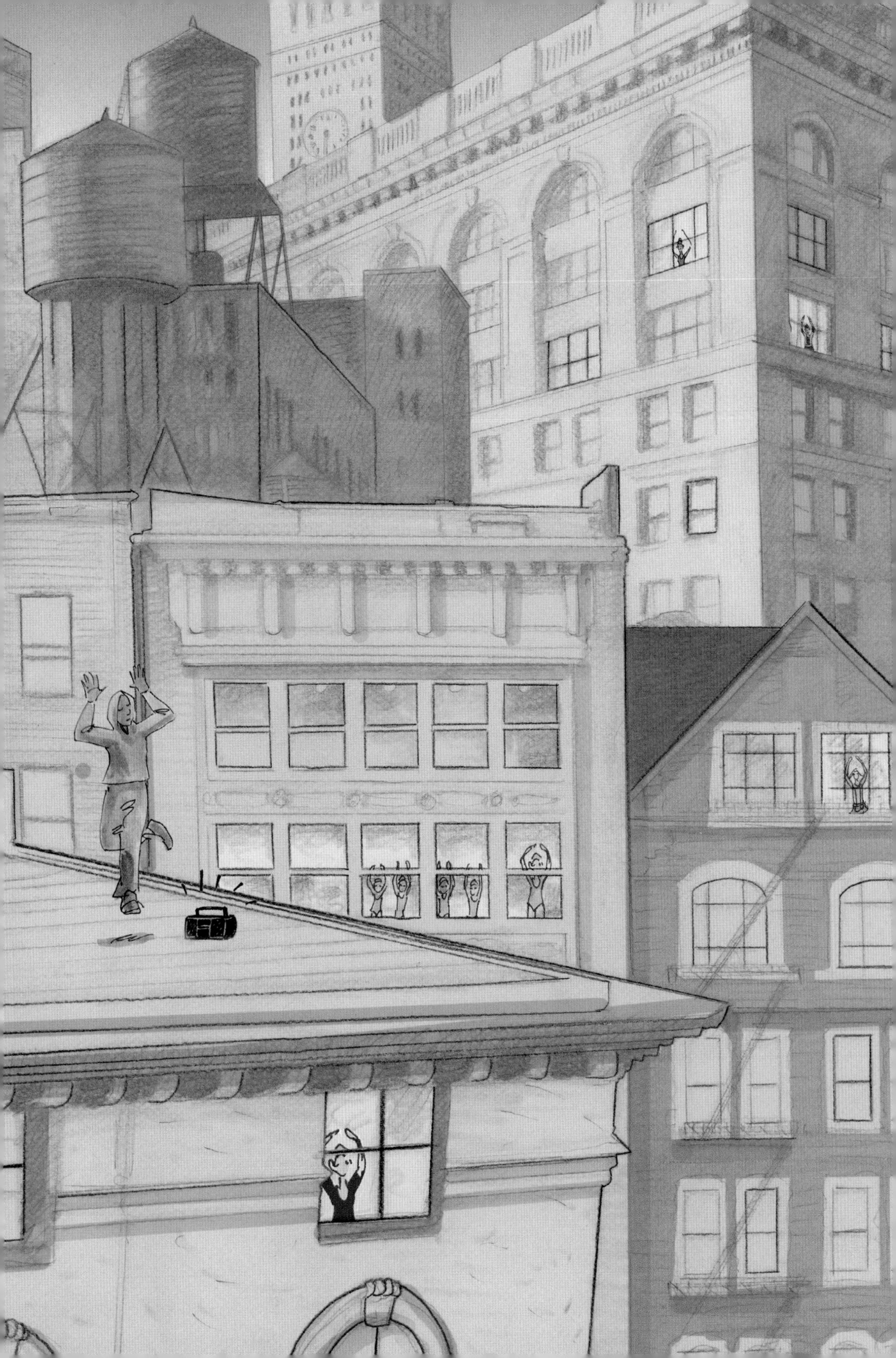

Q: *To Dance* came out in the same year that First Second Books published its first books.

M: Yes, and our first child was born that year too.

Q: How did you go about creating that book?

S: We always thought it would be a graphic memoir.

M: It started with a brief conversation during which we just toyed with the idea and joked about it. One day I mentioned our idea for a "ballet comic" to my editor, a book that would chronicle ten years of Siena's life and be the only ballet book in existence with a football scene, because Siena likes football. Six months later I was talking with my editor again when he said out of the blue, "You know that dance book with Siena? Let's sign it up." He didn't want to see an outline or anything. It was as simple as that.

Q: What did you do first?

M: We had to learn each other's language. I was not especially drawn to ballet. Funnily enough, Siena is like that about comics. Siena had to train me to read a ballet, to teach me the vocabulary of ballet and what to watch for. We saw many performances together—both live and on tape—before finally there was a moment in a grainy old black-and-white video we were viewing that absolutely electrified me. Suddenly I got it! In a similar way, Siena ventured into the world of comics with me.

Siena and I would go for long walks together with a tape recorder running. Eventually, we recorded about a hundred hours of conversations about the story. We wanted a much longer book, but it wasn't a practical option. We kept reworking and reworking the text right up until the end.

S: I don't know how many drafts there were that had to be cut and cut. A graphic memoir I read at the time, and which I would say was a real inspiration for me, was Marjane Satrapi's *Persepolis*.

M: There were certain feelings we were going for. We ended up organizing the story around four key moments. There was the moment when Siena first saw one of the great Russian ballerinas dance and realized how powerful and beautiful dance could be. There was the scene we included from the romantic French ballet *Giselle*. And there was the moment when the great choreographer George Balanchine died, and the moving performance that was given in his memory. Finally, there was the moment when Siena realized she wasn't going to be a dancer.

Q: Mark, how did you settle on the look of the drawings?

M: It was hard. I knew the book needed to have a "feminine" look. I also knew that it's usually pretty painful to look at ballet in the static form of drawings or photographs. I had to find a way to make the drawings fluid. Siena corrected the details: where the elbows and ankles would be, for example. I went for a handcrafted, slightly messy look in the drawings. I wanted them to feel "young" and a little bit light. Throughout the book I drew ribbons like the ones used to tie toe shoes as both a decorative device and a connecting device between sections. I think the ribbons somehow hint at the mystery of dance, which is something that Siena talked a lot about in our taped conversations—the mystery of the connections that dance makes for us that lie beyond words.

Q: Mark, were you involved in web comics?

M: Not until I did *Sailor Twain*. The web comics world is huge, with

This comic about the city as a great honeycomb of shared passions and enthusiasms started out as a one-pager. In the finish, however, the "zoom out" of the final scene has been given a page of its own, the better to tie the whole story together.

millions of readers who don't necessarily also buy books, in part because web comics are so easily forwarded and shared. Some web comics artists would rather raise money on Kickstarter or by selling T-shirts and other merchandise than by having a publishing deal. But not always.

Q: *Sailor Twain* is such a sprawling, big, ambitious book.

M: It took nine years from the time I sketched the first doodles on the commuter train I take to work in the morning! Among the goals I had for myself at the beginning was the idea that I wanted to tell a story from an adult perspective, and that I wanted to make the story layered enough that readers would want to go back to it again and again.

Q: What feeling were you going for in your drawings of the characters? Why, for instance, does Captain Twain have such big cartoony eyes?

M: The story made me do it! Each character is drawn in a different style that reveals something basic about that character's moral view of the world and about his or her inner nature. I drew the captain all in black-and-white and gave him a slightly rigid, geometric look, whereas the more ambiguous Lafayette is more fluid and organic-looking and is drawn in shades of gray. The mermaid, although a fantastic creature, actually looks more naturalistic—more real—than either of the men.

I tried doing the illustrations before choosing to draw them in charcoal, which is very messy and hard to control. But charcoal has such atmosphere. Three strokes and I would have a steamboat appearing out of the mist.

Q: Your drawings remind me of old sepia photographs.

M: I looked at a lot of those old pictures at museums and libraries as I was doing my research, as well as at nineteenth-century maps. I read the diaries of some of the many captains who sailed the Hudson during that period.

Q: What other kinds of research did you do?

M: I set up a *Sailor Twain* website, where I posted one finished page from the book every Monday, Wednesday, and Friday over a period of two years. Eventually, I had posted all of it. As readers discovered the site, it became a shared experience, with a dialogue that grew and deepened.

Every so often there would be somebody who was a total steamboat geek, who knew that the width of the planks in the floor of the captain's room was a bit off and would write to say that the planks would have to be teak or cypress wood, because both are easily replaced in case of water damage. Then they would say, "What were you thinking?!" There was another guy who knew all about engine rooms, who would write comments like "Those pistons are for shallow-water Mississippi steamboats. You've got it all wrong!" It was great to hear from these people.

Q: What did you learn from your experience on the Web?

M: That there's a place now for an author who is an interactive presence and not just a hermit in a cave who tosses out a masterpiece every few years. It's not a hard-and-fast rule, but it has something to do with our time being the age of the Internet.

Early on when the audience was starting to build and I was learning that I needed to respond to what they were saying, I happened to be drawing a crowd scene on board the boat, and so I posted a message that said "Send me a photo and I'll draw you into the scene in 1880s fashion." I thought a few people would do so, but I immediately got seventy-five photos, and they kept coming and coming. By the time I finished the book, I had incorporated cameo portraits of about a hundred readers, or "Twainers," as they started to call themselves, in the illustrations.

Q: Tell me about the comic you created for this book, "City Entity."

S: A city is a mysterious creature. It's a collection of individual homes and people, but it's also an entity. And art is like that too, sometimes individual, sometimes collective. We were especially interested in the idea that any art form—be it in paint, in book form, in film, or in this case in dance—can allow us to become the voice, the instrument, the pen, sometimes without our even being aware of it. So this idea came to us in a conversation: what would it be like if unbeknownst to one another, all the dancers in the city were dancing the same movement at once? What might that release or cause or feel like? Dance, like drawing, can be wordless and open to every individual's own understanding. The feeling of awe and mystery appealed to us and resulted in this strange little comic!

Q: What do you both find particularly satisfying about comics as an art form?

S: Looking back at *To Dance*, I see that Mark was able to capture through his drawings many of the feelings I have about dance that I could not have put into words.

M: I think that, like dance, the best comics touch us on a level that is somehow even more basic than words.

JAMES STURM

(Born 1965, New York, New York)

The heroes of James Sturm's haunting graphic novels are driven people who long to stand apart from the crowd by making their mark in some lasting way. Consider, for instance, the gold miners desperately clambering to strike it rich, as in *Hundreds of Feet Below Daylight;* or, as in *Market Day,* the humble craftsman whose dazzling artistry first enriches his own and other people's lives, then proves powerless to ensure his survival. A love of craft lies at the core of all Sturm's own writing and drawing—and of the graphic novels he admires by others. "So much of the media we consume is mass-produced," he observes, which is a cause of sadness to him. "Comics, or at least the comics I like, feel very intimate. Every mark, from text to image, is hand drawn." In contrast to the *pow!* and *thwack!* of the superhero comics he knew as a child, Sturm lets cartoonish action take a backseat to his protagonists' earthbound struggles to realize their wildest hopes and dreams. As readers, we come to know Sturm's strange characters at disarmingly close range—even those who live in times and places far from our own.

Sturm took his commitment to craft in a different direction in 2004 when he cofounded the Center for Cartoon Studies in White River

Junction, Vermont—an art school dedicated to training students in all aspects of comics creation. As Sturm told me, his own career took off only after it dawned on him that not all comics had to look like *Spider-Man* and the *Fantastic Four*. He had made the discovery by chance, while poring over a college friend's underground comix collection. He takes pride now in encouraging students to find their own way, too.

With well over a foot of newly fallen snow blanketing the ground between Vermont and Brooklyn, we recorded this conversation by phone on the very snowy day of December 17, 2013.

. . . .

Leonard S. Marcus: What were you like as a boy?

James Sturm: Like a lot of cartoonists I've known over the years, I had very few friends, maybe one or two. I always felt a little out of step with any social dynamic. If it was one person, I could deal with it. But if it was a bunch of people, I didn't know how to behave. I was passionate about comics, and I couldn't hide that passion. At school I would be drawing all these funny little doodles of superheroes, and sometimes it was fine and people would look over my shoulder and say, "Draw this. Draw that." By the time I hit high school, I was considered the class artist for sure.

Q: Did you always want to be an artist?

A: The first thing I wanted to be—I was in first grade at the time—was a paleontologist. I loved dinosaur books and especially the illustrations. I can still remember a certain picture of a triceratops battling a *Tyrannosaurus rex*. When we went around the room in class saying what we each wanted to be, I loved saying "Paleontologist." It was the biggest word that any of my classmates had ever heard! Then I realized that if I were a paleontologist, I would have to go out and find dinosaur bones. I thought, "What is the likelihood of *that* happening in suburban New York?" Seeing dinosaurs fighting in a book was not such a huge leap from watching the Hulk battling the Abomination.

Q: How did your passion for comics start?

A: The local newspaper we subscribed to, the *Journal News* of Rockland County, New York, had a comics page. I read *Peanuts* and *Agatha Crumm* and *B.C.* and *Blondie.* I thought they were all great.

Q: What did you like about them?

A: The strips you fall in love with as a kid become real in a way that causes you not to think about the drawing. The story is everything. When I read the comic strip page as a kid, the thing that most impressed me was that the world of each strip felt so different.

Q: Did reading the comics page lead directly to wanting to make comics?

A: I would copy the strips. I was most impressed by the way superheroes were drawn. To me that was "good art." *Peanuts* looked so simple, but when I drew Charlie Brown, he would always look a little off. So I went to the library looking for how-to books.

Then in second grade, three things happened that had a big impact on me. A kids' magazine we got at school called *Dynamite* reprinted *Fantastic Four* number 1. I remember thinking, "Now, *that's* interesting!" Then one day a TV show I watched called *Wonderama* had Stan Lee on as a guest. Lee talked about being a co-creator of the *Fantastic Four.* Not long after that, I found a *Fantastic Four* comic—number 139!—in a pile of used comics in a bookstore in the Paramus Park

Mall, and my parents bought it for me. It was the first comic I owned. I read that thing up and down, and the genie was out of the bottle.

Q: Did your teachers encourage your interest?

A: The art teachers at school didn't consider cartoons to be "real art." My parents signed me up for private art classes, but the teacher had me drawing still lifes, not cartoons. Later, when I was an undergraduate at the University of Wisconsin, an instructor said to me pointedly, "Your comics can influence your art, but they cannot *be* your art."

Q: What did your parents say?

A: My parents were mostly fine with my love of comics. They were just concerned that comics were my *only* frame of reference. I didn't have much passion for anything else, except for the Mets and a couple of other sports teams. I thought, "For now, why not?" I had learned a little German from *Invaders* comics and discovered the Jewish Golem myth from Marvel's *Strange Tales*. The comics were educational! Even when the science in them was only pseudo-science, it got you thinking.

In high school my dream was to draw for Marvel Comics one day. Then I got to college, and my interests expanded a bit while at the same time I began to come to terms with my limitations as a cartoonist. I realized that I couldn't draw the way Marvel needed their superhero figures to look, and I thought that because this was so, I could not be a cartoonist.

Q: Then what happened?

A: I graduated high school in 1983, and I went off to the University of Wisconsin at Madison. I took some art classes, but I also took courses in several other subjects. In my sophomore year, a guy thirteen years older than me moved into the apartment under mine, and we began hanging out together. He liked to play Risk, Monopoly, and poker. We smoked a lot of pot.

He was a geneticist at the university lab and a really brilliant guy, and when he heard I liked comics, he said, "Here, let me show you something." In his apartment he had boxes of underground comix from the sixties. It turned out that his great-uncle was a cartoonist of some renown—Mac Raboy, who drew *Flash Gordon* and *Captain Marvel Jr.*, among others. Years later he gave me his collection as a wedding gift.

What was so great about this is that underground comix were drawn in a million different ways. When I saw that, I realized that I could be a comics artist after all—even though I did not draw in the Marvel superhero way.

At college I drew a five-day-a-week strip for the student newspaper. It was called *The Adventures of Down and Out Dawg.* I was able to see what my work looked like in print, which is really important. I got comments and letters from readers. I would actually see people reading it. It was exciting to draw something, bring it to the office, and have it in print the next day.

I was also trying to do a graphic novel. I wanted to do something serious, to create literature with little pictures, but it wasn't working. I began to read *RAW,* a comics magazine published by Art Spiegelman and Françoise Mouly. Art's *Maus* was being serialized in *RAW* at the time, and I was very inspired by that. From an ad in *RAW* I learned about a graduate program in illustration at the School of Visual Arts, in New York. I applied and got in, and my graphic novel became my major project there. In my second year, I also worked part-time at *RAW*. I got to see the many sketches and drafts that Art had done for each page of *Maus*. I realized how much hard work had gone into making the book look so effortless. That experience really raised my game.

I WAS BORN IN NEW YORK CITY, HOMETOWN OF SO MANY SUPERHEROES. I WAS OBSESSED WITH COMICS GROWING UP AND ANYTIME I WAS IN MANHATTAN I HALF EXPECTED TO CATCH A GLIMPSE OF SPIDER-MAN OR DAREDEVIL SWINGING AMONG THE ROOFTOPS.

TOMORROW, THE WORLD

BY JAMES STURM

IT SEEMED POSSIBLE THAT AN EPIC BATTLE COULD BREAK OUT AT ANY MOMENT!

WAM

SLAM

READING COMICS MADE BEING IN THE CITY MORE EXCITING!

I'VE GROWN UP TO BECOME A CARTOONIST AND NOW LIVE IN A SMALL VERMONT VILLAGE. I DREAM OF CREATING A COMIC THAT AFFECTS THE WAY PEOPLE EXPERIENCE WHITE RIVER JUNCTION . . .

WE HAVE LOCATED THE ONE PLACE ON EARTH OUR PLAN WILL WORK!

LET US SPREAD OUR **PSYCHIC SPORE!**

WE NOW CONTROL THESE HUMANS' BRAINS!

TODAY "THE JUNC," TOMORROW **THE WORLD!**

I'LL HAVE SUCCEEDED WHEN I WITNESS THE FOLLOWING:

...YOU READ TOO MANY COMICS.

I SWEAR, MOM! THEY'RE ALIENS!

WE HAVE TO STOP THEM!!

AND MAYBE THIS KID WILL GROW UP TO BECOME A CARTOONIST TOO!

JS
WRJ
2013

Q: **Did you like living in New York? In the cartoon you drew for this book you make Manhattan out to be the natural home of superheroes.**

A: Cartoonists spend a lot of time alone. It's very jarring when you're suddenly dropped into the middle of a city where there are a million things to notice. When I was in graduate school, it was months before I could have a conversation with somebody while walking down the street because I would be in a constant state of distraction: noticing the architecture, overhearing bits of conversation, listening to all the different languages being spoken, stopping to see what books were for sale from all the street vendors. And if you've been in the studio all day struggling to draw something in particular—say, people in winter jackets—when you go out, you are looking intently at every winter jacket you see and how it's constructed and put together.

Growing up, I had gone into the city all the time with my parents. We visited my grandmother and my parents' friends, went to Broadway shows and museums. At the American Museum of Natural History, I would race through the galleries to get to the giant model of the blue whale hanging from the ceiling, floating in space. That was so incredible to me.

Q: **Your first graphic novel was *The Revival*, a story based on historical fact about a Christian faith healer who traveled the American frontier. What drew you to your subject?**

A: I was living in Seattle at the time and had just started seeing a woman who was a psychic healer. She was able to see the inside of your body the same as if she was telling you the color of your shirt. She knew things about people that were impossible to know. This was also the time of the Internet boom, when some people thought the Internet was going to save the world. They had so much faith in what technology might achieve. Making a book about a revival was my way of asking, What *is* possible? What are the limits of faith? It's not entirely clear whether or not the girl in the story was helped by the faith healer. Readers have interpreted the ending both ways. I like it when a story is left a bit open-ended.

The Revival was the first of three historical graphic novels that were later collected as a trilogy called *James Sturm's America.* The second one, *Hundreds of Feet Below Daylight,* was about a mining town in frontier Idaho. *The Golem's Mighty Swing* was the third story. The Golem book was a way for me to touch base with my own origins as a Jew. Having done so much research for *The Revival,* I felt I knew more about Christianity in America than I did about Judaism. Also, I wanted to ask the question: What *is* an American? We're proud to be a "nation of immigrants," but the real question is: When you come to this country, what do you have to leave behind and what do you need to keep with you? A story about a Jewish exhibition baseball team seemed like a good way to get at this question. In the first half of the book, the characters are baseball players first, Jews second, in an almost incidental way. But in the second half, the situation is reversed when they become involved with a promoter who takes out newspaper ads for them, writes stories about them in the papers, and has an African American man on the team pose as the legendary Golem. Media attention has a way of amplifying stereotypes. All of a sudden the players are Jews first—and scary Jews at that in the minds of many—which leads to some really bad consequences for the team.

Also, I saw something very Jewish in baseball. Every year at the Passover table, Jews say, "Next year in Jerusalem." Judaism is all about getting back home. In baseball you step up to home plate, and the object of the game is to circle the bases and return home.

Q: In *The Golem's Mighty Swing,* when the promoter Mr. Paige snaps his attaché case shut, you have the word "click" floating in the air of the panel. What makes comics sound-effect words like that one so interesting?

A: It comes at the end of a scene and at a turning point in the story. It is a way of adding a beat for emphasis. Comics are pictures that you read, images that function like language. The reverse of that is that text can be turned into a part of the picture. The play between those elements can be exciting. And when you have a sound effect—"click"—suddenly language starts to function as an image. That's one of the things that is so cool about comics.

Q: Soon after the Golem book, you finally got your old wish and drew a story for Marvel.

A: I had an idea for a story that I wanted to tell, and when I approached Marvel, the editor knew my Golem book, which had gotten a lot of attention, and he gave me the opportunity to write a four-issue miniseries. *Unstable Molecules* was an extension of all the historical fiction I had been doing lately. The *Fantastic Four* had been created in the early sixties. Just as the legend of Johnny Appleseed was based on a real person named John Chapman, I pretended that the *Fantastic Four* was based on real-life fifties characters and that I was revealing the backstories of these four supposedly real people. The events described in *Unstable Molecules* all take place during one weekend in 1959. They show the powers of each superhero character manifesting from who they were as individuals and as people of their time. For example, there's a passage in Jack Kerouac's *On the Road* that reads something like: I want to go up into the sky and burn, burn, burn like a roman candle. When I read that, I thought, "That sounds like the Human Torch!" So I began to think of the Human Torch as a fifties teenager. I decided he would have been a beatnik and that he would definitely have read and been inspired by *On the Road*! I saw in the Invisible Girl an image of what girls were expected to be like in the fifties, before the feminist movement.

Q: In *Market Day* you told another story rooted in Jewish history, this time with a setting in Eastern Europe in the early 1900s.

A: I initially thought of *Market Day* as a testament to the character called Albert Finkler. Here's this guy who runs his shop at a loss just so that he can give support and encouragement to the artists whose creations he sells. He brings artists together and makes them feel worthwhile. But as the story evolved, it came to be more about Mendleman, the talented rug maker who, when Finkler's shop is taken over by others, suddenly has to face the artist's very common dilemma that there may not be people who care about his work.

Q: How did you find your drawing style?

A: This is a hard question to answer. For the longest time, I would see something by another artist that I admired and try to integrate it into my work. But I always came back to my own way of drawing, which I think is pretty straightforward. I'm not going to wow anyone with my electric brushwork or dynamic compositions, but I do feel that I can articulate what needs to be articulated in a simple and pleasing manner. My intent with my art is not to attract attention to the drawing but rather to effectively tell the story I am driven to tell.

Q: How are graphic novels like film? Or are they?

A: It can be a valid analogy up to a point. You can talk about individual drawings in a graphic novel in terms of "shots" and "close-ups."

James Sturm's sketches are so expressive that when viewed side by side with the finishes, it is as though we are getting two slightly different but equally satisfying versions of the same story.

At the same time, the best comics could only be comics. With a film, you are almost always looking at only one image at any given time. But with comics, you are taking in an entire page at a time, and you can go back, or stop, or go forward as you choose. You can look at the whole page.

Also, comics have their own visual rhythms. If you have a nine-panel grid, you can decide that every other panel is going to be a talking head and that the other panels will have different subjects.

Curiouser and curiouser: for some reason, the little boy seen calling out the aliens in this sketch has become a little girl in the finish.

Each panel is a discrete unit of time. When you string them together, one next to the other in a certain order, that's what makes a comic go.

From panel to panel, you can shift from someone's memory, to that person's aspiration, to the current moment. Past, present, and future can coexist on a single page. If you break out of a regular pattern of panels, it starts to mess with your notion of time a little bit. That's unique to comics.

Q: You have done a lot to encourage other artists, both as the cofounder of the Center for Cartoon Studies and as the author of the Adventures in Cartooning books.

A: Everyone draws as a kid, but most kids stop at a certain point. The number-one reason they stop is the huge gap that starts to develop between what they are able to create versus what they are consuming. They love *Toy Story* or *Spider-Man,* and what they draw is so far from that that they say, "I'm not good at this." Adventures in Cartooning is meant to give kids characters and a story they can easily copy. It gives them some notches on their artistic belt so that when they try to jump the artistic chasm between what they're able to do and what they aspire to be, they'll have enough enthusiasm to make it across.

Q: Do you have a work routine?

A: *(Laughter.)* No, I have two kids. One is thirteen, and the other is eleven. I help run a school and I have all my projects, so I am generally very busy. From the inside out, it doesn't *feel* as though I have a very disciplined routine. Deadlines really help, though.

Q: Would you say something more about the comic you created for this book, "Tomorrow, the World"?

A: When I saw that the theme of the comic was "the city," I immediately thought about the comics I loved as a kid like the *Fantastic Four* and *Spider-Man.* New York City was such an essential element of these comics. Somehow a guy who was bitten by a radioactive spider becomes more credible when the city he is swinging through is real.

Q: The second part of your comic looks more like Vermont, where you live now.

A: Over the years I've called Savannah, Philadelphia, Seattle, Bozeman, and Madison, Wisconsin, home. In each of these places, the people, the landscape, and the history provided a wellspring of inspiration. I finally settled in Vermont because I had long dreamed of starting a cartooning school, and White River Junction seemed like the ideal place to do just that. So in that regard, my "fantasy" became a reality.

Q: What do you like best about making graphic novels?

A: I like owning my own characters—as opposed to what happens when you work for a company like Marvel. And I like having the opportunity to explore certain themes in a novelistic way. I like being free to decide halfway through to change everything, and not having anybody to tell me not to do it.

SARA VARON
(Born 1971, Chicago, Illinois)

Sara Varon's official web biography, all of one sentence long, is as modest as Varon herself is in person, but with none of the sly, self-deprecating humor that quickly seeps into her conversation. Asked once how, as the illustrator of Cecil Castellucci's *Odd Duck,* she had been able to get so thoroughly inside the head of the story's fussbudget heroine, Varon, noting a certain resemblance in herself to Theodora, replied, "Well, I feel like a weirdo, you know."

Theodora and her seriously annoying next-door neighbor Chad are not only metaphorical odd ducks but real ducks, too. Other Varon comics feature a dog, a cat, a robot, a cupcake, and an eggplant. Humans have yet to make their appearance in her published books, in part because she believes she does not draw people all that well. Knowing her limitations, it seems, has long played a key role for Varon in honing in on her strengths. In her early books—*Robot Dreams* and others—she told stories entirely in pictures because, she says, she did not consider herself a strong writer then either.

Varon's droll, brightly painted characters could be toys and edibles come to life on the page. But their emotions are unmistakably human, as are their reactions to the classic predicaments they routinely find themselves in, difficulties revolving around the kinds of conflicts that inevitably arise between friends, and the fallback choices that present themselves when things do not go as originally planned."

Varon has also put her delightfully deadpan characters to use for a variety of handcrafted objects; in addition to the small throw rug that lies at the center of her living-room floor and the T-shirts she likes to make for friends, there are now also greeting cards, zipper bags, and necklaces featuring lions, monkeys, birds, and her dogs, among others.

Varon lives in a cozy brick row house in Brooklyn, New York, not far from an old-fashioned elevated train station. We recorded our conversation in her living room on November 11, 2013.

• •

Leonard S. Marcus: What kind of child were you?

Sara Varon: Quiet and awkward. Nerdy probably. I liked animals, and we had dogs. I liked to draw, and I drew characters all the time. I had one character that I drew for a couple of years. I made stories with pictures about the people I knew in school for my friends, and they thought they were funny. I've always doodled little characters.

Q: Did you read comics growing up?

A: No, I didn't. I knew about the superhero comics, but I didn't like them. I saw *Archie* in the supermarket, but the girls were so girly that *Archie* didn't interest me either.

Q: Did you always want to be an artist?

A: I studied biology briefly at college but dropped out. If I wasn't an illustrator, I would have liked to be a vet.

Q: When you enrolled in art school, what sort of artist were you hoping to become?

A: At the beginning I didn't think about it. I studied animation as an undergraduate because I had loved television cartoons when I was growing up. But cartoons are hand drawn, and so labor-intensive. I spent three years working on a six-minute film called *The Tongue*, which nobody could see because it had to be shown on a projector. I sat in my room tracing pictures for three years. It was cool to bring your characters to life and see them move. But after that experience, I said to myself, "I can't do this again!" So I became a printmaker, which I think served me pretty well later when I started making books. As a printmaker, I learned about color and about what works in print and what doesn't.

Q: How did you find your way into the world of graphic novels?

A: While I was still in college, I worked for a designer in Chicago who had an amazing library that included some graphic novels. From him, I learned that whenever you need a new idea, a good thing to do is to look at lots of books. I was browsing in his library when I discovered graphic novels for myself. I think the first one I read was *The Dum Dum Posse* by Ron Regé Jr. I hadn't seen anything like that before, and I thought it was exciting. When I found those first comics that interested me, I started drawing more like them. And I realized that graphic novels and comics were a sort of shorthand for animation.

Q: How do you come up with your characters?

No Place Like Home

by Sara Varon

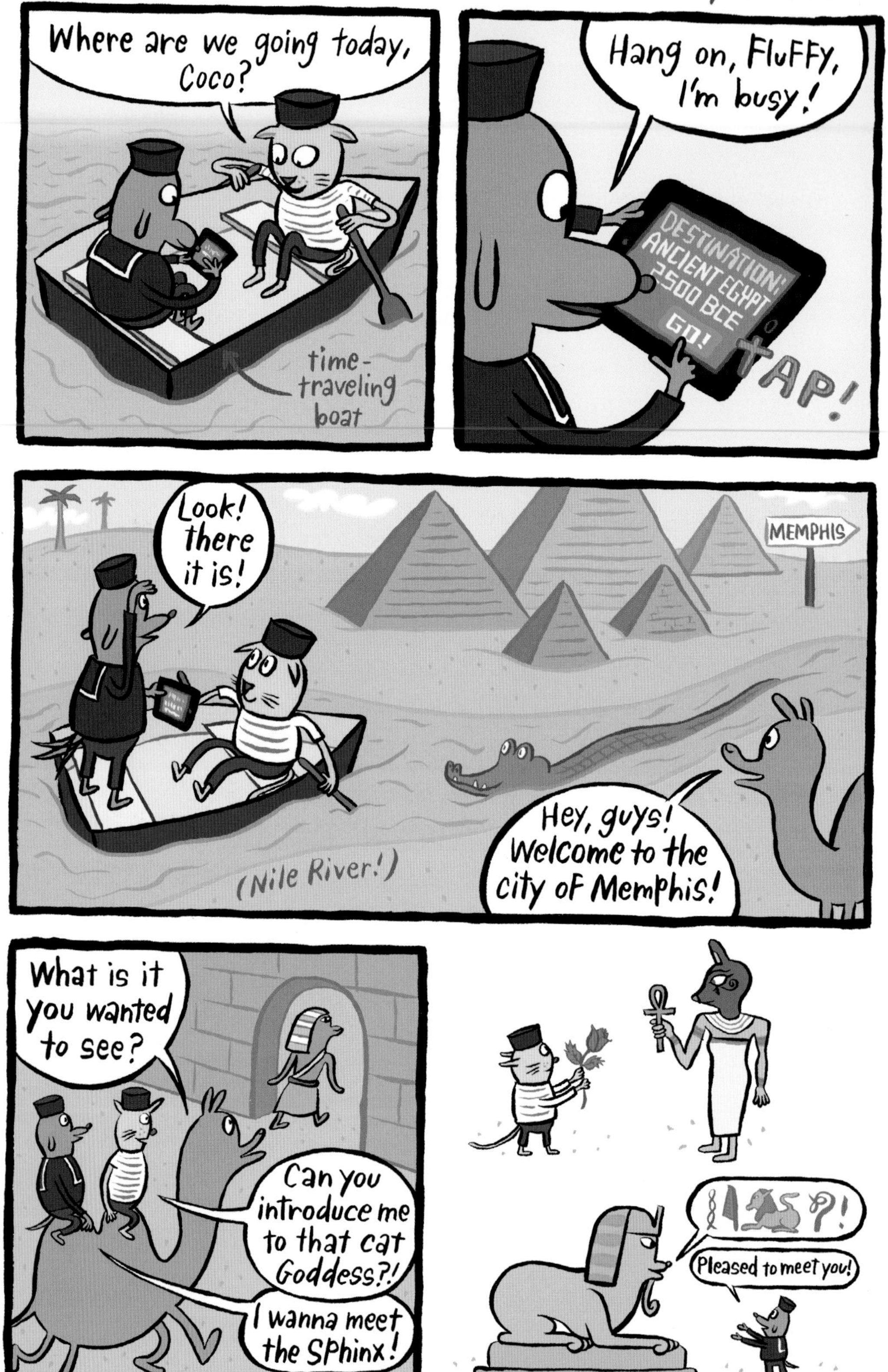

Where are we going today, Coco?
time-traveling boat
Hang on, FluFFy, I'm busy!
DESTINATION: ANCIENT EGYPT 2500 BCE
GO!
TAP!
Look! there it is!
MEMPHIS
Hey, guys! Welcome to the city of Memphis!
(Nile River!)
What is it you wanted to see?
Can you introduce me to that cat Goddess?!
I wanna meet the SPhinx!
Pleased to meet you!

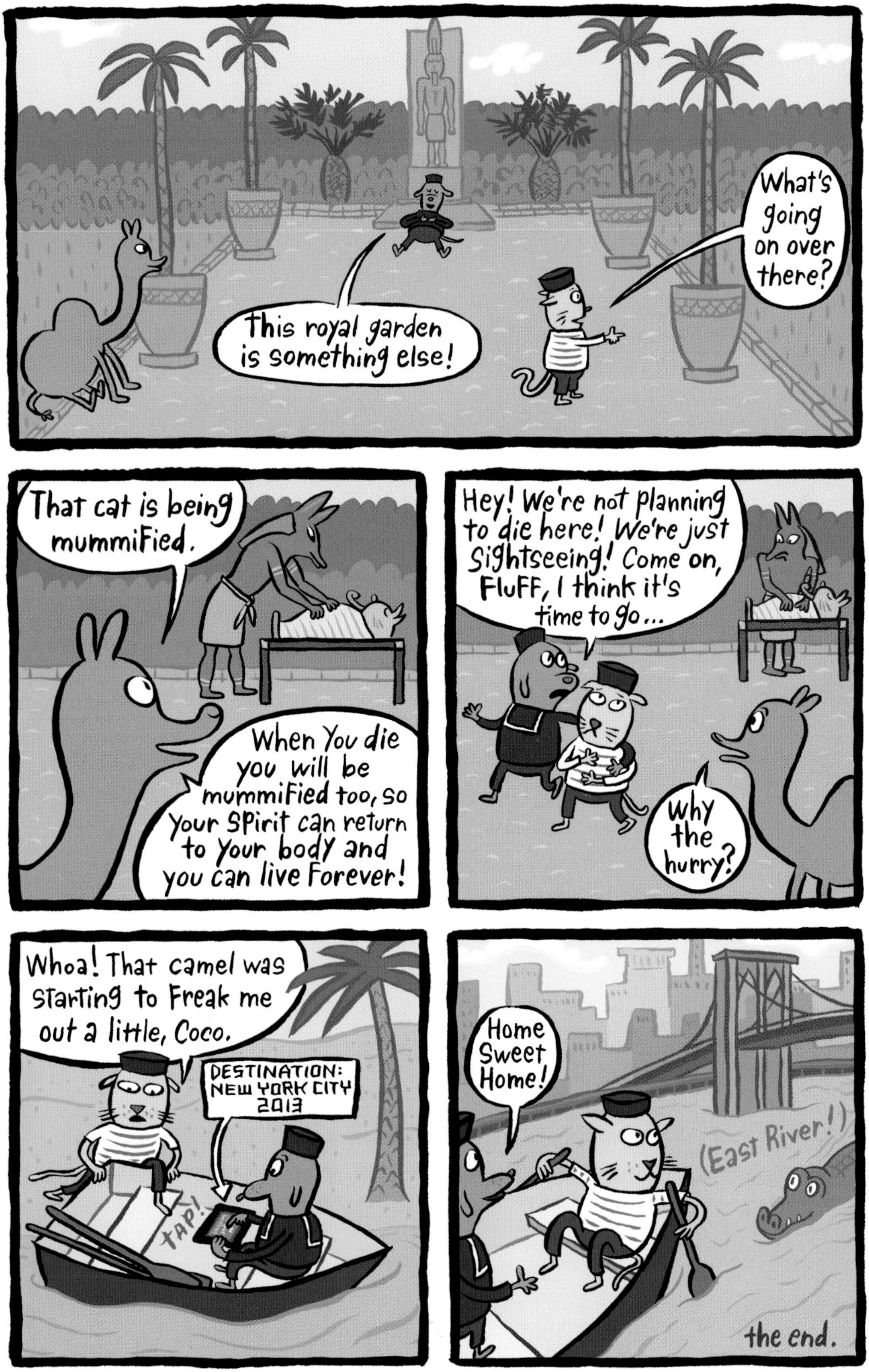
This royal garden is something else!
What's going on over there?
That cat is being mummified.
When you die you will be mummified too, so your spirit can return to your body and you can live forever!
Hey! We're not planning to die here! We're just sightseeing! Come on, Fluff, I think it's time to go...
Why the hurry?
Whoa! That camel was starting to freak me out a little, Coco.
DESTINATION: NEW YORK CITY 2013
TAP!
Home Sweet Home!
(East River!)
the end.

A: I found a big white paint chip in the street in my neighborhood one day, in Williamsburg, Brooklyn, that had come off a wall. Someone had scribbled legs and a beak on it with a marker. I really liked the spontaneity of that drawing. It inspired me to make up a chicken character of my own that became one of the friends in my first picture book, *Chicken and Cat.*

Q: What gave you the idea to make a cupcake character for your book *Bake Sale*?

A: About ten years ago, I had a coworker for whom I wanted to make a T-shirt as a present. We both really liked cupcakes, and so I drew a cupcake character on the shirt, and I liked it enough to think about putting it—him—in a story. At that time I wanted very much to go to Turkey. I had wanted to go there for years because in an art history class I took at the Art Institute we had studied Hagia Sophia, the Greek Orthodox basilica in Istanbul, and I wanted to see it for myself. Travel is expensive, but if you make a project about your trip, you can write it off on your taxes! So I tried to figure out a story that linked Turkey to Cupcake. Finally, I came up with the story for *Bake Sale,* and I did go to Turkey. My plan had been to take pictures while I was there and make my drawings based on the photographs. But when I got to Turkey, I felt that I couldn't draw it because it was all *so* different and because I realized that I couldn't really get to know it in a short amount of time. Istanbul is packed with millions of things, and a lot goes on there. That is why in *Bake Sale* my character ends up not getting to go to Turkey after all—because I felt that I could not represent it well enough.

Q: You set the comic you made for this book, "No Place Like Home," in Egypt. You must enjoy traveling.

A: Yes, I do like seeing new places, and a journey to someplace new is a good start for a story because it means your characters have left behind their regular routines and may be ready for an eye-opening experience, an adventure.

The book I'm working on now is a travel story too. My husband is from Guyana, and my new book takes place there, in a little village populated entirely by animal characters: dogs and chickens and sheep and stuff. In Guyana, animals are wandering around every-where. Most of them seem to belong to people, but during the day the cows roam around on their own. I saw a lot of donkeys there. My main character is a donkey. I like it when things don't really make sense, and you have to say, "Oh, it's just a story, so I'll go with it." Anything can be believable. My characters all have spaghetti arms—even the birds! In my new book, the donkey has a guidebook to animals. The animals look realistic in the guidebook's illustra-tions, but not the "real" ones who live in the village.

Q: Do you think of your books as experiments? Do you set out each time to do something you have never done before?

A: Sometimes I do, but the experiment does not always go as planned. I wanted my new book, the one set in Guyana, to be a mystery. I was remembering the feeling of the Nancy Drew books I had read grow-ing up. As it turned out, the story I wrote was not a mystery at all. But it *is* an adventure story, which is also something new for me.

Before *Odd Duck,* I hadn't done a story with words. *Chicken and Cat* and *Robot Dreams* were both wordless books. So when I did *Odd Duck,* which is written by Cecil Castellucci, I had to figure out how to work with words. After that experience, I finished *Bake Sale,* the first book I wrote and illustrated. So *Odd Duck* was a stepping-stone.

Q: Are there artists you especially admire now?

A: Among graphic novelists, I admire Aaron Renier because he draws

Sara Varon edits herself in the margins.

so well and Anouk Ricard for her playful way of drawing. Among picture book artists, I love everything about the books of William Steig: his loose, scratchy line, his characters. They're funny and silly and also somehow meaningful. You identify with his characters and can understand what they're thinking about and what their concerns are. *Doctor De Soto* is my favorite.

While her playful drawings always bring a smile, these sketches also show how carefully designed and drawn they are.

Q: Is there anything you cannot draw?

A: I'm not very good at drawing people. I have never drawn people, and I still don't. If I draw a dog, it's a generic dog, and people will all look at it and think, "That's a dog." But it's hard to catch a human likeness. There are other reasons for having animal characters. I can draw a rabbit and color it green, and color another rabbit pink, and no one will question it because it's pure fantasy. But if I draw a green person, people will ask, "Why? What's going on?" Another good reason for animal characters is that anybody can relate to a dog or cat or rabbit character. Because it's not necessarily young or old, or male or female, this makes the character more widely accessible.

Q: In *Bake Sale*, Cupcake talks about the famous baker named Turkish Delight as a great artist. Do you think that baking is like making art?

A: No, actually. I don't think of baking as very creative, except when you're decorating, because it's so orderly. You're following a recipe. It's more science-y than arty. With art you want to be evolving and progressing all the time.

Q: How have you changed as an artist?

A: It took me a while to learn to paint with a brush. It's hard to use a brush, but the more I did it, the more control I had over it. It has a nice flowing quality that I usually like. I am interested now in getting better at lettering. I hand letter when I can. I hand lettered *Odd Duck*. I think hand lettering looks so much better than type and allows the letters to become a part of the drawing, which is important.

Q: Do you revise your work?

A: I do a thumbnail, then I do the drawings in pencil, and then I go on to the finish. I feel that drawing something over and over again takes the life out of it, so I like to draw an illustration as few times as possible. Sometimes I move things around later—an arm, a leg—in Photoshop.

Q: Do you have a work routine?

A: I am orderly except about working. Right now Monday and Wednesday are my drawing days because I have a part-time job. I'll do dishes and eat lunch four times a day just so that I don't have to get to work. I guess I love to procrastinate!

Q: What do you like about making your books?

A: Some of the first graphic novels were pretty bleak, but that's not my thing. I feel that if you can bring something into the world, it should be something that will make people happy rather than bring them down. I hope that's not too fluffy! I think my books are comical. I know I'm entertaining myself when I make them.

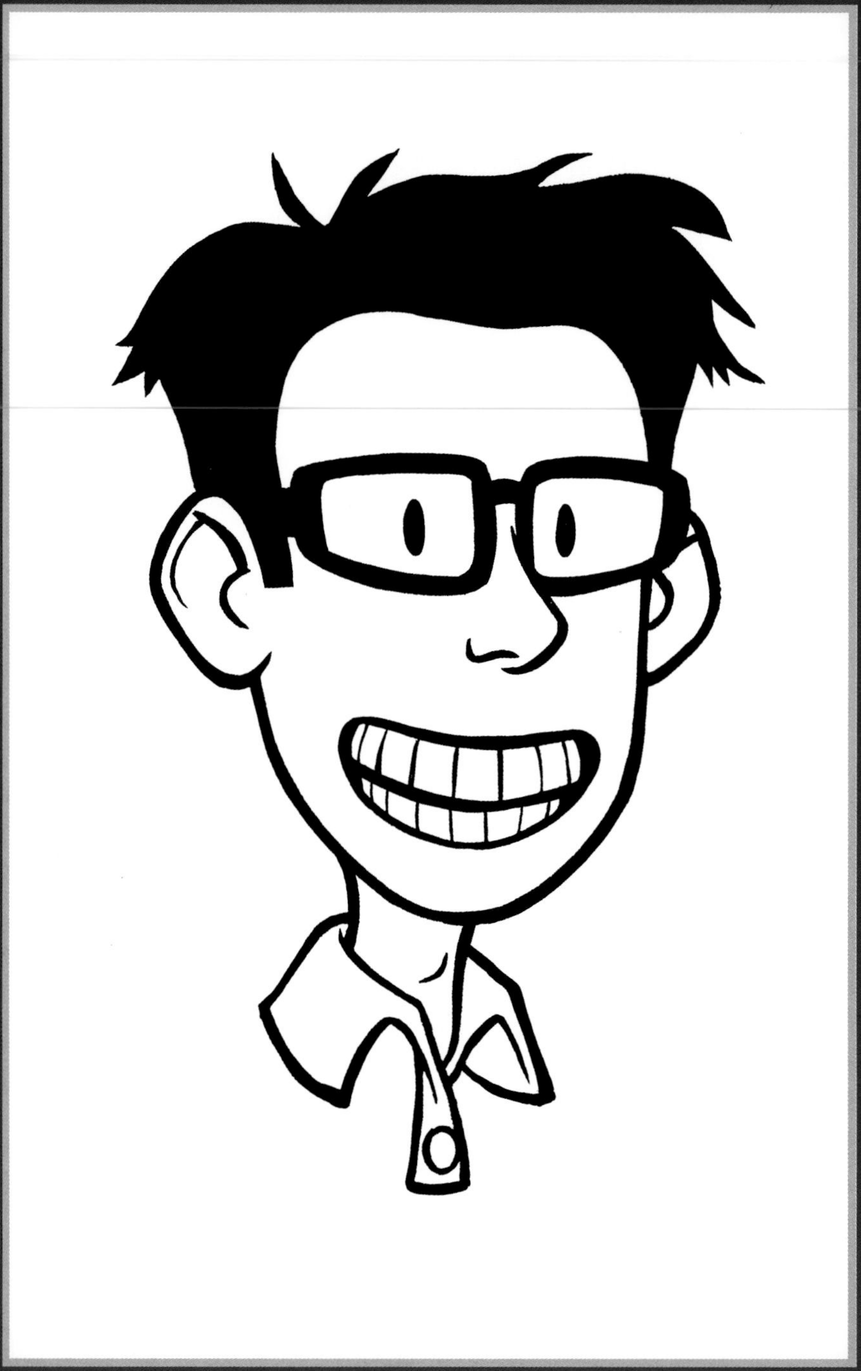

GENE LUEN YANG
(Born 1973, Alameda, California)

As a third-grader, Gene Yang had dreams of being a Disney animator. By fifth grade he had discovered *Superman* and switched allegiances, but the fantasy of blasting out a place for himself in the comics universe had if anything grown stronger than ever. That same year he wrote and drew his first comic book. It was enough to wrinkle the brow of his earnest, hardworking father, who urged him to study something "practical" in college.

Yang majored in computer engineering while also taking writing classes at UC Berkeley and continued to draw. After graduation he was glad he had followed his father's advice and was able to support himself—first as a programmer, then as a teacher—as he published his first stories with tiny, obscure imprints like Humble Comics (really, Yang himself) and Slave Labor Graphics, and hoped that fans would find them.

Both Gene's parents were Chinese immigrants, and like millions of others before them, they had struggled to feel at home in America. As a schoolchild, Yang also learned that life as a member of a minority culture could be confusing and painful, even in a country that proclaimed itself open to everyone. He thought long and hard about what it meant to be an American *and* a person of Chinese heritage, and this became the subject of his first major graphic novel, *American Born Chinese*. A landmark book, it received the Michael L. Printz Award for teen fiction and was nominated for a National Book Award—two firsts for a graphic novel.

Yang is a boyish, modest man with a quick laugh and an easygoing manner. As a storyteller and artist, however, he works on the grand scale whether he is exploring a tumultuous time in modern Chinese history, as in *Boxers & Saints,* or constructing a parallel universe as a coauthor of *Avatar: The Last Airbender,* the continuation in book form of a popular Nickelodeon television series that he had first loved as a fan.

Yang was home in northern California when we spoke by phone on January 3, 2014.

• •

Leonard S. Marcus: What were you like growing up?

Gene Luen Yang: I was pretty classically geeky. I was not very good at sports. I spent a lot of time writing and drawing and watching cartoons. I had thick glasses. Because I had respiratory problems, I carried an inhaler. I fit the geek stereotype to a T!

Q: How did you find your way into the world of comics?

A: Both of my parents are avid storytellers. I loved listening to them. So I grew up loving stories. I also grew up drawing. My mom tells me that I started drawing when I was two years old. Early on I found myself wanting to combine storytelling and drawing. I had my heart set on becoming a Disney animator. Then in fifth grade, I started collecting comics. The first one I bought was DC Presents number 57: *Superman and the Atomic Knights,* a story about an atomic war and its aftermath. It was awesome! A friend and I would get our parents to drive us both to the library. After they drove away, we would walk together to a local comics store about twenty minutes away. We would buy comics out of the quarter bin, then return to the library, where we would check out the biggest books we could find—to hide our comics in. Nowadays you can find all sorts of comics in the library, but when I was growing up, there were few if any.

Q: What did your parents think of comics?

A: They did not like them, especially my dad. He was very traditional in his thinking and had read an article about how comics were bad for kids, how the stories were terrible for us, and how the lettering, because it was so small, would cause eye strain. That's why we had to hide the comics in order to get them into the house. Eventually, my parents gave up on trying to stop me from reading comics and tolerated it.

Q: Were you a good student?

A: I did OK in school, not a bad student but also not a superstar. I had a hard time reading any book that I was required to read. If a book was assigned, I automatically found it difficult. But if later I read the same book on my own—*To Kill a Mockingbird* is a good example—I would often find that I enjoyed it.

Q: Was your home bilingual?

A: Yes. We spoke mostly Mandarin at home. I do so even now with my parents, even though my Mandarin isn't very good. It feels weird to speak to them in English. My little brother, who is four years younger, and I spoke Mandarin until he was in junior high and I got to the point where there were things I could not express to him in Mandarin. That is when we switched over. At first that felt weird too.

Q: Did your parents want you to think of yourself as Chinese or American or what?

A: Both impulses were there. They wanted us to be successful in America. At the same time, they sent us to Chinese school and celebrated traditional Chinese holidays.

Q: How did you feel about your Chinese heritage?

A: I went through phases. When I was really little, I liked traditional Chinese stories, especially those about the Monkey King, which my mom read to me from books. I loved those! As I got older, I realized how my cultural heritage was different from that of most of the kids at school, and by fifth or sixth grade, it became something that I wanted to get away from. There were very few Asian Americans in our local public schools when we first moved into our neighborhood when I was very young. Later that changed, and I lived through the transition. When I got to junior high, we were still a minority, but a large-enough group that there were a couple of cliques of Asian American kids who hung out with each other.

Q: Did you experience prejudice like that which you describe in _American Born Chinese_?

A: Yes. In junior high people are insecure, and a lot of ugly stuff can come out. I put much of what I heard in the hallway in junior high into _American Born Chinese_. It was just a small minority of students who would say those things, but, given my own insecurity at that age, I would wonder whether _all_ of my non-Asian classmates saw me the way those few highly vocal kids did. That was when I started feeling really awkward about hanging out with non-Asian kids. They all seemed to be perfectly nice people. But I would always wonder what they were thinking.

Q: Laurence Yep is an author who for a time wrote science-fiction stories about alien creatures because, as a Chinese American, he felt himself to be an alien in the cultural sense.

A: Maybe that's one of the reasons that I gravitated toward comics. When I was growing up, most comics were about superheroes, and in superhero stories you have the idea of balancing identities. The hero will have two different lives that have to be balanced. In a way that is what an immigrant's kid has to go through too. Most of us speak two different languages. We might even have two different sets of clothes and two different sets of names. I have one name that I would be called at home and another name—Gene—that I would be called at school.

Q: Did you study Chinese brush painting?

A: We learned calligraphy at Chinese school, but I was never very good at it.

Q: In *American Born Chinese,* your character Chin-Kee is a very exaggerated caricature. Has anyone objected to that character, even though it is clear that your intent was to call out an offensive stereotype?

A: Dave Chappelle played with offensive black stereotypes on *Chappelle's Show* in order to show how ridiculous they were. I think I wanted to do something similar. But when you play with stereotypes, it is always a little dangerous. There is always the chance that someone will misread your intention. I have had that experience very occasionally. That's why *American Born Chinese* is best thought of as a young adult book rather than one for younger kids.

Q: Chin-Kee is, among other things, the Chinese superstar student that some non–Chinese Americans fear are winning too many prizes and scholarships.

A: Right. I wanted to take a bunch of stereotypes, both modern ones and some from the past, and combine them in one character. I grew up around some of those stereotypes. For instance, in DC Comics there was a character called Egg Fu, who was a human-size yellow egg from China with a big Fu Manchu mustache, and there was the Mandarin, a mad scientist and martial arts master. Both characters were supposedly created just for laughs.

Q: You dedicated *American Born Chinese* to your parents. You thank your mother for telling you Monkey King stories and your father for telling you stories about a Taiwanese village boy. What were your father's stories like?

A: My dad would make up stories off the top of his head for my brother and me. Most of them were about a little boy named Ah-Tong, who I think was kind of a stand-in for my dad. He would take stories from his childhood and play them up a bit to make them funnier. The ones that I liked the best were about the really disgusting chores that Ah-Tong's dad would make him do, like going to the front of the house and having to clean up cow manure. I think some of what happened in the stories was real.

Q: I read that you have an aunt who does Chinese brush painting.

A: She is my mother's older sister and has been an inspiration to me. I always think that my interest in drawing comes from my mom's side of the family. My aunt didn't start painting until she was an adult, and when she did, she learned how to paint by taking a correspondence course. She has had exhibitions and is really very accomplished. It's pretty amazing that she was able to get so far in those circumstances.

Q: In *American Born Chinese,* you have a haunting line that is spoken to the Monkey King as a kind of warning and rebuke: "You may be a king — you may even be a deity — but you are still a monkey."

A: When I was in high school, I did a pen-and-ink drawing of the Monkey King for an art class. When I brought it home and showed my mom, she took one look at it and said, "You did it wrong!" I wasn't expecting that, so I asked, "What did I do wrong?" She pointed to the feet of the Monkey King and said, "The Monkey King always wears shoes, and you drew him barefoot." When I asked her why the Monkey King would wear shoes, my mom replied, "To hide the fact that he's a monkey, because he's ashamed of being a monkey." I thought that was a powerful idea: that deep down, this being, despite all his many superpowers, could still be ashamed of who he was. I thought that was a good way to talk about the discomfort that immigrant kids sometimes feel. No matter how American your clothes look, no matter how good your English is, there's always going to be something that makes you different.

Q: Why did you name the high school in *American Born Chinese* "Oliphant"?

A: I named it after Pat Oliphant, who is a famous American political cartoonist. In 2001 he drew a cartoon that commented on what had become one of the year's big news stories, prior to 9/11. An American spy plane had gone down in or near Chinese airspace,

Berkeley, California

by Gene Luen Yang

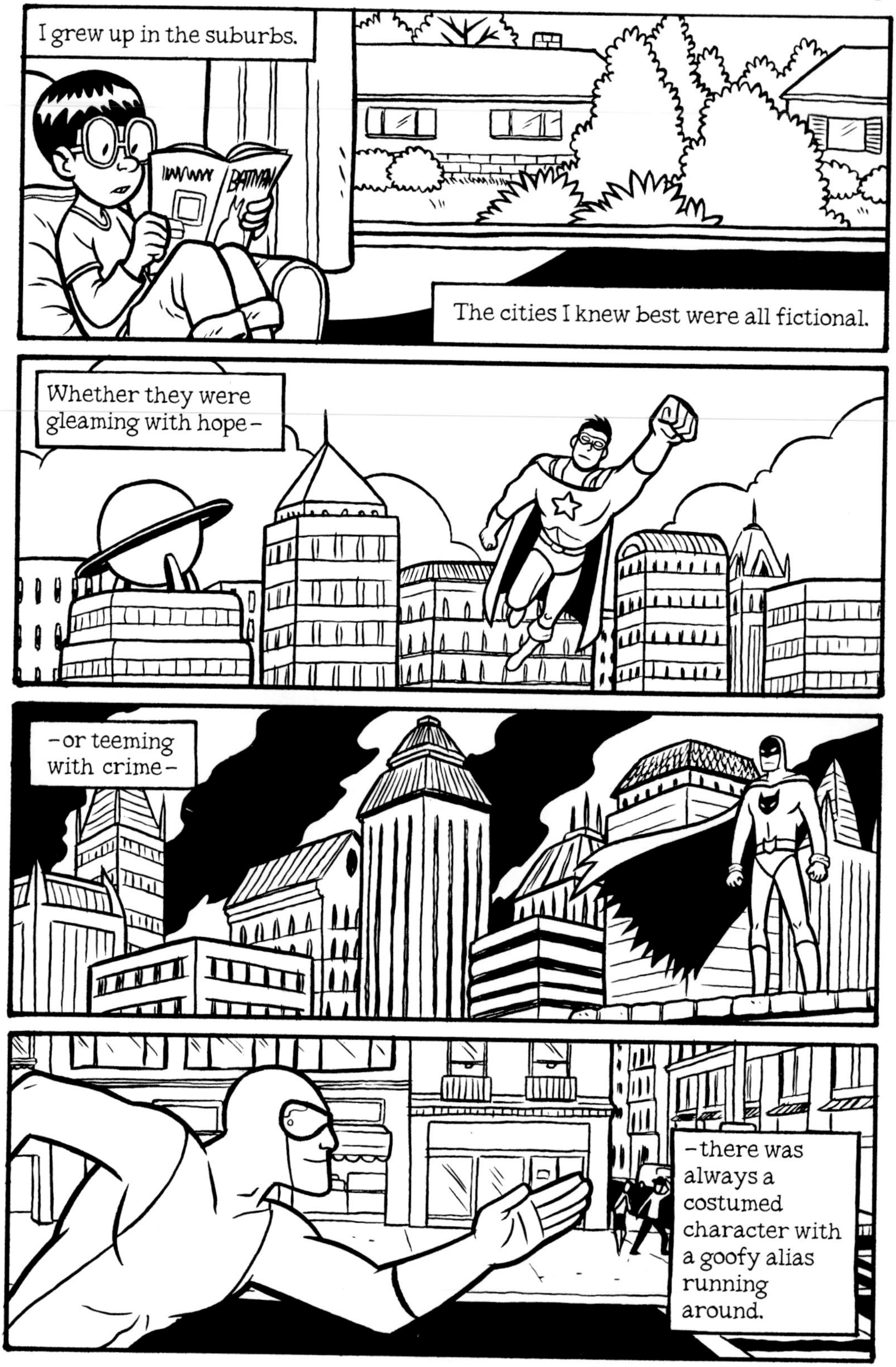
I grew up in the suburbs.
The cities I knew best were all fictional.
Whether they were gleaming with hope –
– or teeming with crime –
– there was always a costumed character with a goofy alias running around.

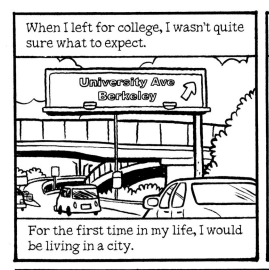

When I left for college, I wasn't quite sure what to expect.

University Ave Berkeley

For the first time in my life, I would be living in a city.

I found Berkeley, California, to be a noisy, passionate, colorful place.

I immediately fell in love.

It wasn't all that different from the cities of my comic books.

HATE YOUR MOM LUKE 14:26

Pink Man

Naked Guy

Hate Man

resulting in a major diplomatic crisis. In Oliphant's cartoon, Uncle Sam is seen going into a Chinese restaurant and being served a plate of crispy fried cat gizzards with noodles. The waiter has really slanty eyes and buckteeth—a lot like Cousin Chin-Kee in *American Born Chinese*. When I saw that in my local newspaper, I was a little shocked that somebody would be doing that sort of thing in 2001. I thought there would be a reaction, that maybe the artist would be asked to apologize—but it didn't happen. Oliphant's caricature was a little subtler than those found in the old turn-of-the-century cartoons, which I think that people in mainstream America today would immediately recognize as offensive. But Oliphant was drawing from the same well, and so I named the high school after him.

Q: You dedicated *Boxers* to "the original art night crew." Who were you thinking of?

A: They are a group of cartoonists who all used to live in the Bay Area. When we were in our early and mid-twenties, we would hang out together once a week at somebody's house to draw and critique each other's stuff and talk shop. We called it art night, and it went on for years and years. I never went to art school, and I consider those gatherings my art school.

Q: What did you study in college?

A: I majored in computer science and minored in creative writing. UC Berkeley didn't have a comics major, or I would have done that instead.

Q: Were you writing stories like the ones you are known for now?

A: In high school I had written an essay about race that was inspired by Jonathan Swift's satire "A Modest Proposal." That's when I first got interested in satire as a way of talking about my own world. In college I did some autobiographical writing, bits and pieces of which filtered into *American Born Chinese*. But I wasn't writing comics yet.

In college I was debating between becoming a Disney animator or doing comics after I graduated. I eventually chose comics because I felt that that medium gave you more control over the story. Animators almost never have much control.

Q: Why do you think comics have become so popular?

A: A lot of it has to do with how good the work has been. Art Spiegelman's *Maus* was a big deal. The fact that *Maus* won a Pulitzer Prize was a big deal too. Marjane Satrapi's *Persepolis* was a *New York Times* bestseller. It was a big deal to see that comics could have that kind of success. Scott McCloud's *Understanding Comics* meant a lot to my friends and me. After reading that book, I stopped thinking of comics only in terms of superheroes and realized that the comics format could be a container for any kind of story I wanted to tell. With all this happening, more and more people began to take comics seriously and to push the medium.

Q: Is the story of the Boxer Rebellion part of your own family history?

A: Within my own family, my mom was the convert to Catholicism, so Western faith does go that far back for us. But I grew up in the Chinese Catholic community, and I think for Christians of Chinese descent, the Boxer Rebellion still has a special resonance because it embodies the old conflict between Eastern culture and Western religion. Nowadays, being Chinese and Christian is not generally seen as conflicting, but a century ago that was not the case.

Several of the priests who served in the church I grew up in had grown up in China and had been imprisoned by the Communist government. So the idea of faith and country being in conflict with each other and the idea of suffering for your faith were both very real to me through the stories they told.

Q: Why did you want to tell the story of the Boxer Rebellion?

A: I first got interested in the Boxer Rebellion in 2000, when Pope John Paul II canonized a group of Chinese Catholic saints. It was the first time the Roman Catholic Church had acknowledged the Chinese in this way, and it was treated as a big deal within my home church. We had all sorts of celebrations and masses and awesome food! The festivities inspired me to look into the lives of these newly canonized saints. What I discovered was that many of them had been martyred during the Boxer Rebellion because they were seen as traitors to Chinese culture—traitors to their country.

Q: Toward the end of *Boxers*, you show the destruction of China's greatest library.

A: When I found that story during my research, I knew it would be one of the big moments in the book. It encapsulated everything that I felt about the Boxers. I felt that I understood where the Boxers were coming from. I sympathized with them. I could see that at that time Chinese culture needed defending. Yet the Boxers ended up destroying a great library, a great repository of Chinese culture—the very culture that they had set out to defend.

Q: Mei-wen says, "What is China but a people and their stories?"

A: That's really what any culture boils down to: human beings and the stories we tell. My view of the Boxers is that their stories were incomplete. Chinese folklore also has tales of deep compassion. Those stories the Boxers ignored.

Q: Do you see a connection between your work with computers and your work as an author?

A: My next book will be about computers. And I do think there's an overlap between the two disciplines in which I've worked. Programming is sequential. It's all about taking complex ideas and breaking them down into simple lines of code. Comics are like that too. You can take a complex story and break it down into themes, and then into panels. The panels have to be simple enough that a reader can follow them easily. At the same time, you hope that ultimately all these panels will add up to something that is rich and complex.

Q: What are the steps in the process of making a book?

A: With *Boxers & Saints,* I started with research, reading everything I could about the Boxer Rebellion. Eventually I moved on to writing a script. Then I broke the script up into panels for which I also made sketches. Then I made detailed pencil drawings for each panel, and then the inks. Next I scanned my inks into the computer. The pages are lettered and colored on the computer.

Q: Is there anything that you cannot draw?

A: Oh, yes! I have a hard time with horses. I have to draw them over and over again. Crowd scenes are hard for me. It takes me a long time to do perspective correctly. The female form is hard, possibly because I grew up drawing male superheroes. Almost anything is hard.

Q: How did your work as a coauthor of the Avatar series come about? What has it been like to help extend a story that you first knew as a fan from the *Avatar* television show?

This initial sketch, which differs in only minor details from the finish on page 157, was drawn digitally.

A: A friend of mine introduced me to Nickelodeon's *Avatar: The Last Airbender* television show, and by the third episode I was hooked. In my opinion, it's the best cartoon series America has ever produced.

Around the time the show ended, Nickelodeon announced the live-action movie adaptation. At first I was excited. I couldn't wait to see sky bison rendered in 3-D. Then they announced the casting.

Avatar: The Last Airbender is set in a fantasy world, but it's a fantasy world based on real-world Asian and Inuit cultures. It's obvious—at least to me—that all the characters are meant to be either Asian or Inuit in appearance. In the live-action adaptation, all the major heroic roles were played by white actors. It was the latest example of yellowface, Hollywood's long-standing practice of taking roles that would most logically go to actors of color and giving them to white actors.

I was mad, so I made a web comic about it. One of the people who read my web comic was an editor at Dark Horse Comics. A couple of years ago, after Dark Horse acquired the Avatar: The Last Airbender license from Nickelodeon, that editor asked if I'd be interested in writing the Airbender graphic novels for them. Of course, I said yes. Basically, I got the gig by complaining.

I've been working on the Airbender books for a few years now, and it's been an amazing experience. I get to work closely with Mike DiMartino and Bryan Konietzko, the creators of the original series. They're phenomenal storytellers, and I've learned so much.

Q: Do you have a work routine?

A: Nowadays I spend every other day working on comics. It also depends on what part of the process I'm in. If I'm drawing, I try to finish one or two pages a day. Writing is not as time-consuming, but it is more soul wrenching for me. At the end of some days, I'll feel I have barely gotten anywhere. Other days I will have done a lot. Writing is harder to plan.

Q: What was the thought behind the comic you created for this book?

A: The comic is an homage to two things that are close to my heart: superhero comics and the city of Berkeley. Both are colorful, both are misunderstood, and both have profoundly affected my life.

Q: What do you find most satisfying about making comics?

A: I like being part of a global storytelling community. Collectively, stories are a kind of giant conversation about what it means to be human. It's nice to be able to participate in that conversation.

SOURCE NOTES

HARRY BLISS

p. 2: "*Nancy* and *Blondie* spoke to me": e-mail to author dated December 4, 2013.

GEOFFREY HAYES

p. 23: "fortif[ied]" and "inner world": Geoffrey Hayes, "Rory," in *Where Demented Wented: The Art and Comics of Rory Hayes,* edited by Dan Nadel and Glenn Bray (Seattle: Fantagraphics, 2008), p. 132.

p. 24: "I still believe we can never have too much sweetness": e-mail to author dated December 2, 2014.

KAZU KIBUISHI

p. 39: "I believe a lot in focusing on just a few things": Natalie Zutter, "Kazu Kibuishi reimagines 'Harry Potter' covers," posted on *Bookish,* August 13, 2013.

p. 40: "Every time I do a new book": ibid.

p. 40: "It hurts my hands when I look at it": Scott McCloud quoted in "Kazu Kibuishi," posted on comicbooksdb.com.

HOPE LARSON

p. 54: "I went to ice cream school": Hope Larson, "Classic Graphic Novel: Why I Adapted 'A Wrinkle in Time,'" posted on *Huffington Post,* September 21, 2012.

DANICA NOVGORODOFF

p. 67: "'DC or Marvel?'": Danica Novgorodoff, "Where I Get My Inspiration," posted on *Huffington Post,* June 12, 2014.

DAVE ROMAN

p. 95: "Yes!": Vincent M. Mallozzi, "Blank Comic Book Page Told the Whole Story," *New York Times,* October 15, 2011, p. A17.

JAMES STURM

p. 121: "So much of the media we consume is mass-produced": quoted in Will Wilkinson, "Thinking in Comics: A Roundtable on the Present and Future of the Graphic Novel," in *Gulf Coast: A Journal of Literature and Fine Arts,* Winter/Spring 2014, pp. 133–158.

SARA VARON

p. 137: "Well, I feel like a weirdo, you know": Antonia Saxon, "Q & A with Cecil Castellucci and Sara Varon," posted on *Publishersweekly.com,* May 16, 2013.

ART MEDIA NOTES

HARRY BLISS
Self-portrait (p. xvi): Black ink and graphite
"Up, Up, and Away" (p. 5): Black ink and graphite
Preliminary drawings (p. 9): Black ink and graphite

CÁTIA CHIEN
Self-portrait (p. 12): Graphite and charcoal on paper
"Water" (pp. 18–19): Graphite and charcoal on paper
Preliminary drawings (p. 21): Graphite and charcoal on paper

GEOFFREY HAYES
Self-portrait (p. 22): LePen with digital color
"Mister Bear Makes His Move" (pp. 28–29): Copic Multiliner brush pen and colored pencils on Strathmore drawing paper
Preliminary drawings (pp. 34–35): HB pencil on heavy weight copy paper

KAZU KIBUISHI
Self-portrait (p. 38): Photoshop and Wacom Cintiq
"Copper" (pp. 44–45): Pencil on paper for line-work, Photoshop CC and Wacom Cintiq for color
Preliminary drawings (pp. 48–49): Pencil on paper; blue color pencil on paper.

HOPE LARSON
Self-portrait (p. 52): Brush and ink on Bristol
"Starland" (pp. 60–61): Brush and ink on Bristol, colored in Photoshop
"Starland" drawings (pp. 64–65): The first and only preliminary drawing, modified at the time of the addition of color

DANICA NOVGORODOFF
Self-portrait (p. 66): Ink and watercolor on paper
"Turf" (pp. 72–73): Ink, watercolor, and digital color
Preliminary drawings (pp. 76–77): Ink on paper

MATT PHELAN
Self-portrait (p. 80): Pencil and watercolor on paper
"City Life" (pp. 86–87): Pencil and watercolor on paper
Preliminary drawings (pp. 90–91): Pencil on paper

DAVE ROMAN

Self-portrait (p. 94): No. 2 lead pencil and Speedball Super-Black India ink applied with Winsor & Newton Series 7 sable brush on Strathmore 500 Series surface Bristol paper, with color added in Photoshop on a Wacom tablet, and captions and speech balloons lettered in Yaytime

"The Proximity Effect" (pp. 100–101): No. 2 lead pencil and Speedball Super-Black India ink applied with Winsor & Newton Series 7 sable brush on Strathmore 500 Series surface Bristol paper, with color added in Photoshop on a Wacom tablet, and captions and speech balloons lettered in Yaytime.

Preliminary drawings (p. 105): No. 2 lead pencil on paper

MARK SIEGEL

Self-portrait and portrait of Siena Cherson Siegel (p. 108): Ink and watercolor on paper

"City Entity" (pp. 112–113): Pencil, graphite, and charcoal with digital color

Preliminary drawings (p. 116): Pencil on paper

JAMES STURM

Self-portrait (p. 120): Pencil on paper

"Tomorrow, the World" (pp. 126–127): Pen (Speedball c-5 and c-6 nibs), brush (Pentel brush pen and/or No. 2 sable brush), and ink, colored in Photoshop

Preliminary drawings (pp. 132–133): Pencil on paper

SARA VARON

Self-portrait (p. 136): Brush pen and ink on Xerox paper, colored in Photoshop

"No Place Like Home" (pp. 140–141): Brush and ink on Bristol, colored in Photoshop

Preliminary drawings (pp. 144–145): Pencil on Xerox paper

GENE LUEN YANG

Self-portrait (p. 148): Pen and ink

"Berkeley, California" (pp. 156–157): Photoshop

Preliminary drawing (p. 162): Photoshop

SELECTED READING

HARRY BLISS

Bliss (syndicated one-pane comic). Chicago: Tribune Media Services, 2005–present.

Death by Laughter. New York: Abrams, 2008.

Luke on the Loose. New York: TOON, 2009.

CÁTIA CHIEN

"Fall" and "Tumbleweed," in *Flight,* vol. 1, edited by Kazu Kibuishi. Berkeley, CA: Image, 2004.

"Jelly Fruit," in *Flight,* vol. 2, edited by Kazu Kibuishi. Berkeley, CA: Image, 2005.

Princess Alyss of Wonderland (written by Frank Beddor). New York: Dial, 2007.

GEOFFREY HAYES

Benny and Penny in the Big No-No! New York: TOON, 2009.

Benny and Penny in Just Pretend. New York: TOON, 2008.

Benny and Penny in Lights Out! New York: TOON, 2009.

Benny and Penny in Lost and Found! New York: TOON, 2014.

Benny and Penny in the Toy Breaker. New York: TOON, 2010.

Patrick Eats His Peas. New York: TOON, 2013.

Patrick in a Teddy Bear's Picnic and Other Stories. New York: TOON, 2011.

KAZU KIBUISHI

Amulet: The Stonekeeper, vol. 1. New York: Scholastic, 2008.

Amulet: The Stonekeeper's Curse, vol. 2. New York: Scholastic, 2009.

Amulet: The Cloud Searchers, vol. 3. New York: Scholastic, 2010.

Amulet: The Last Council, vol. 4. New York: Scholastic, 2011.

Amulet: Prince of the Elves, vol. 5. New York: Scholastic, 2012.

Amulet: Escape from Lucien, vol. 6. New York: Scholastic, 2014.

Amulet: Firelight, vol. 7. New York: Scholastic, 2016.

Copper. New York: Scholastic Graphix, 2010.

Daisy Kutter: The Last Train, book 1. Irving, TX: Viper Comics, 2005.

Explorer: The Hidden Doors (editor). New York: Abrams, 2014.

Explorer: The Lost Islands (editor). New York: Abrams, 2013.

Explorer: The Mystery Boxes (editor). New York: Abrams, 2012.

Flight, vols. 1–8 (editor, 2004–11).

Flight Explorer. New York: Villard, 2008.

HOPE LARSON

Chiggers. New York: Atheneum, 2008.

Compass South (illustrated by Rebecca Mock). New York: Farrar, Straus and Giroux, 2016.

Gray Horses. Portland, OR: Oni Press, 2006.

Madeleine L'Engle's A Wrinkle in Time: The Graphic Novel (adapted and illustrated by Hope Larson). New York: Farrar, Straus and Giroux, 2012.

Mercury. New York: Atheneum, 2010.

"Weather Vain," in *Flight,* vol. 2. Berkeley, CA: Image, 2005.

Who Is AC? (illustrated by Tintin Pantoja). New York: Atheneum, 2013.

DANICA NOVGORODOFF

Refresh, Refresh (adapted from the screenplay by James Ponsoldt; based on the short story by Benjamin Percy). New York: First Second, 2009.

Slow Storm. New York: First Second, 2008.

The Undertaking of Lily Chen. New York: First Second, 2014.

MATT PHELAN

Around the World: Three Remarkable Journeys. Somerville, MA: Candlewick, 2011.

Bluffton: My Summers with Buster Keaton. Somerville, MA: Candlewick, 2013.

"Jargo!," in *Sideshow: Ten Original Tales of Freaks, Illusionists, and Other Matters Odd and Magical,* edited by Deborah Noyes. Somerville, MA: Candlewick, 2009.

Snow White. Somerville, MA: Candlewick, 2016.

The Storm in the Barn. Somerville, MA: Candlewick, 2009.

DAVE ROMAN

Agnes Quill: An Anthology of Mystery (illustrated by Jason Ho, Raina Telgemeier, and others). San Jose, CA: SLG, 2007.

Astronaut Academy: Re-Entry. New York: First Second, 2013.

Astronaut Academy: Zero Gravity. New York: First Second, 2011.

"The Chosen One," in *Flight,* vol. 5. New York: Ballantine, 2008.

Goosebumps: Slappy's Tales of Horror (co-illustrated by Dave Roman; written by R. L. Stine). New York: Parachute, 2015.

"The Great Bunny Migration," in *Flight,* vol. 3. New York: Ballantine, 2006.

"It's Dangerous to Sleep," in *Flight,* vol. 4. New York: Ballantine, 2007.

The Last Airbender (coauthored by Dave Roman and Alison Wilgus; illustrated by Joon Choi). New York: Del Rey, 2010.

The Last Airbender: Prequel: Zuko's Story (coauthored by Dave Roman and Alison Wilgus; illustrated by Nina Matsumoto). New York: Del Rey, 2010.

Teen Boat! (illustrated by John Green). New York: Clarion, 2012.

Teen Boat: Race for Boatlantis, illustrated by John Green. New York: Clarion, 2015.

MARK SIEGEL

Sailor Twain: or, The Mermaid in the Hudson. New York: First Second, 2012.

Seadogs: An Epic Ocean Operetta (written by Lisa Wheeler). New York: Atheneum/Richard Jackson, 2004.

MARK SIEGEL AND SIENA CHERSON SIEGEL

To Dance: A Ballerina's Graphic Novel. New York: Atheneum/Richard Jackson, 2006.

JAMES STURM

Adventures in Cartooning: Activity Book! (co-created with Andrew Arnold and Alexis Frederick-Frost). New York: First Second, 2010.

Adventures in Cartooning: Characters in Action! (co-created with Andrew Arnold and Alexis Frederick-Frost). New York: First Second, 2013.

Adventures in Cartooning: Christmas Special (co-created with Andrew Arnold and Alexis Frederick-Frost). New York: First Second, 2012.

Adventures in Cartooning: Gryphons Aren't So Great (co-created with Andrew Arnold and Alexis Frederick-Frost). New York: First Second, 2015.

Adventures in Cartooning: Hocus Pocus (co-created with Andrew Arnold and Alexis Frederick-Frost). New York: First Second, 2016.

Adventures in Cartooning: How to Turn Your Doodles into Comics (co-created with Andrew Arnold and Alexis Frederick-Frost). New York: First Second, 2009.

Adventures in Cartooning: Sleepless Knight (co-created with Andrew Arnold and Alexis Frederick-Frost). New York: First Second, 2015.

Birdsong. New York: TOON, 2016.

James Sturm's America: Gold, God, and Golems. Montreal: Drawn & Quarterly, 2007. [Note: this volume comprises three previously published books: *The Revival, Hundreds of Feet Below Daylight,* and *The Golem's Mighty Swing.*]

Market Day. Montreal: Drawn & Quarterly, 2010.

Satchel Paige: Striking Out Jim Crow (illustrated by Rich Tommaso. New York: Hyperion, 2007.

Unstable Molecules (Fantastic Four Legends, vol. 1, illustrated by Guy Davis). New York: Marvel, 2003.

SARA VARON

Bake Sale. New York: First Second, 2011.

Chicken and Cat. New York: Scholastic, 2006.

Chicken and Cat Clean Up. New York: Scholastic, 2009.

Odd Duck (written by Cecil Castellucci). New York: First Second, 2013.

President Squid (written by Aaron Reynolds). San Francisco: Chronicle, 2016.

Robot Dreams. New York: First Second, 2007.

Sweaterweather. Cupertino, CA: Alternative Comics, 2003. Reissued as *Sweaterweather and Other Short Stories.* New York: First Second, 2016.

GENE LUEN YANG

American Born Chinese. New York: First Second, 2008.

Avatar: The Last Airbender: The Promise (coauthored with Michael Dante DiMartino and Bryan Konietzko; illustrated by Gurihiru). Milwaukie, OR: Dark Horse, 2013.

Avatar: The Last Airbender: The Rift (coauthored with Michael Dante DiMartino and Bryan Konietzko; illustrated by Gurihiru). Milwaukie, OR: Dark Horse, 2015.

Avatar: The Last Airbender: The Search (coauthored with Michael Dante DiMartino and Bryan Konietzko; illustrated by Gurihiru). Milwaukie, OR: Dark Horse, 2014.

Avatar: The Last Airbender: Smoke and Shadow (illustrated by Gurihiru). Milwaukie, OR: Dark Horse, 2015.

Boxers & Saints. New York: First Second, 2014.

The Eternal Smile: Three Stories (illustrated by Derek Kirk Kim). New York: First Second, 2009.

Level Up (illustrated by Thien Pham). New York: First Second, 2011.

Secret Coders. New York: First Second, 2015.

The Shadow Hero (illustrated by Sonny Liew). New York: First Second, 2014

ACKNOWLEDGMENTS

Thanks first and foremost to the artists and writers who took part in this project, graciously giving of their time and talent. I also wish to thank the following individuals, who provided invaluable help along the way: Gina Gagliano, Reilly Hadden, Judy Hansen, Edite Kroll, Kate R. Kubert, Holly McGhee, Tanya McKinnon, David Saylor, and Mark Siegel.

I am grateful to my editors at Candlewick Press, Deborah Noyes, Carter Hasegawa, and Katie Ring, and art director Sherry Fatla for their consummate professionalism and good fellowship at every turn. And I thank my agent, Erica Rand Silverman, and her colleague at Sterling Lord Literistic, Caitlin McDonald, for their continuing friendship and guidance.

Finally, a tip of my hat to the two artist-provocateurs from whom I learned to love the comics form: Jules Feiffer and the original *Mad* man, the late Harvey Kurtzman.

INDEX